The Extraordinary Life of E. Nesbit

This book is dedicated to my loving husband.

The Extraordinary Life of E. Nesbit

Author of *Five Children and It* and
The Railway Children

Elisabeth Galvin

PEN & SWORD
HISTORY

First published in Great Britain in 2018 by
PEN AND SWORD HISTORY
an imprint of
Pen and Sword Books Ltd
47 Church Street
Barnsley
South Yorkshire S70 2AS

ISBN 978 1 52671 477 0

Printed and bound in the UK
by T J International, Padstow, Cornwall, PL28 8RW

Typeset in Times New Roman 10.5/13.5 by
Aura Technology and Software Services, India

Pen & Sword Books Ltd incorporates the imprints of Pen & Sword
Archaeology, Atlas, Aviation, Battleground, Discovery,
Family History, History, Maritime, Military, Naval, Politics, Railways,
Select, Social History, Transport, True Crime, Claymore Press,
Frontline Books, Leo Cooper, Praetorian Press, Remember When,
Seaforth Publishing and Wharncliffe.

For a complete list of Pen and Sword titles please contact
Pen and Sword Books Limited
47 Church Street, Barnsley, South Yorkshire, S70 2AS, England
E-mail: enquiries@pen-and-sword.co.uk
Website: www.pen-and-sword.co.uk

Contents

Edith Nesbit's Family Tree

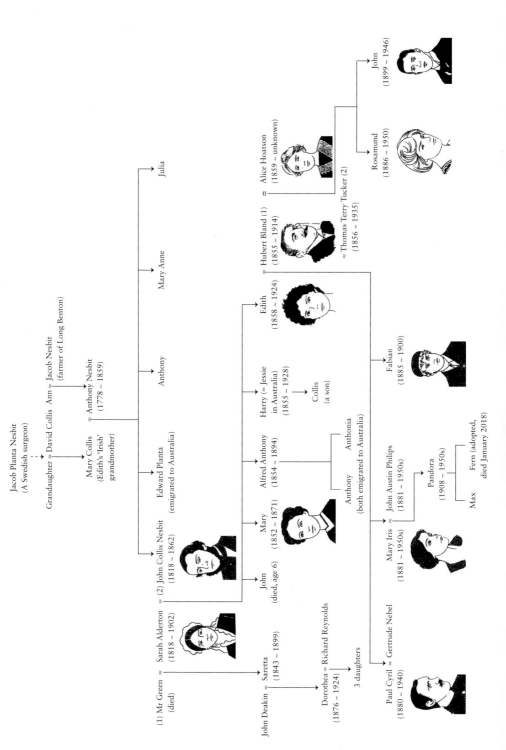

Acknowledgements

The painstaking work carried out by Edith Nesbit's two previous biographers Doris Langley Moore OBE and Professor Julia Briggs resulted in comprehensive archives of irreplaceable historical material that are invaluable to anyone writing about Edith Nesbit. Seven years after the author died, Mrs Langley Moore undertook, as a young writer who had recently moved out of London, the monumental task of documenting the life of a deeply unconventional woman. The fact that Mrs Langley Moore wrote some thirty letters alone attempting to uncover the reason for Hubert Bland's conversion to Catholicism indicates her extraordinary commitment to research, and she admitted to putting her heart and soul into the project. Without her efforts, much of Edith's personal history would have been lost forever. Some of the facts that Mrs Langley Moore uncovered were thought inappropriate to be revealed so soon after Edith's death and were left out of *E Nesbit: A Biography*, which was published in 1933 by Ernest Benn (the publisher Edith shared). However, she revised her book thirty-three years later in 1966, to include a more complete picture of her subject. In the 1980s, she graciously gave her notes and contacts to help Professor Julia Briggs write a new biography – a gesture that the always-generous Edith would have approved. The result was that Prof Briggs left no stone unturned in her unsurpassed biography *A Woman of Passion*, published in 1987 by Penguin Books. As a pioneer in the study of children's literature, Prof Briggs' conscientious research into Edith's life couldn't have been more comprehensive nor her analysis of her findings more intelligent.

Edith Nesbit was keen throughout her career to help up-and-coming writers, and as a first-time author, I found this deep generosity in abundance in Dame Jacqueline Wilson who so very kindly wrote the foreword to this book and also agreed to be interviewed. I will always be grateful for her support, encouragement and enthusiasm; she is an E. Nesbit for the twenty-first century. Similarly, Kate Saunders was the first person I interviewed for the biography and her great knowledge, passion and intellectual understanding of Edith Nesbit gave me the best start I could have asked for.

ACKNOWLEDGEMENTS

The warmth and friendship I have received from the Edith Nesbit Society has been invaluable, particularly the assistance of Margaret and Jerry McCarthy, Marion and John Kennett, Margaret Taylor, Maureen and Brian Speak, Bronwen and Ian Fair and Fern Ravandi, Edith Nesbit's great-granddaughter who is an honorary member of the Edith Nesbit Society, www.edithnesbit.co.uk.

Special thanks must go to Jenny Agutter and Bernard Cribbins for very kindly being interviewed. Also, Mike Kenny, Caroline Harker and David Barron (along with Laura Elmes at Runway Entertainment) who were part of the production of *The Railway Children* at Waterloo Station and King's Cross Theatre and generously agreed to speak with me after I saw the play in its last week in January 2017.

I would also like to thank the Biographers' Club and I. Marc Carlson and staff at the Department of Special Collections, McFarlin Library, The University of Tulsa, Oklahoma, United States of America for their help with the Edith Nesbit Collection.

Further thanks must go to Jo Mahoney at Prendergast School; Niky Stonehill of StonehillSalt PR for her help with the chapter on *Harry Potter;* and to Tracey Grove for introducing us. Celia Catchpole of the Catchpole Agency very generously and conscientiously read through the manuscript and made invaluable suggestions, as did my friends including Elena Dalrymple, Georgina Wilczek and Kirsty Nancarrow. My greatest gratitude goes to my family for their enthusiasm, practical support and constant encouragement especially Bob and Helen Galvin, my husband Brad and my three young children Mary, William and Elsa. My warmest acknowledgement must go to my sister, Hayley Relph, who read the book twice before publication, and to my parents, Bert and Gay Attwood, who first read me *The Railway Children* and inspired my lifelong love of literature.

Foreword
Dame Jacqueline Wilson

I'm delighted to be introducing a new biography of Edith Nesbit, my favourite children's author. A handful of her wonderful books are still in print, even though they're more than a hundred years old, and there have been television adaptations, films and stage shows – but most people know very little about Edith herself. Perhaps it's because all her children's books called her E. Nesbit on the title page, a stark and sexless name that gives away nothing.

There's a lot to be told about Edith's private life. Indeed, her first biographer, Doris Langley Moore, had to be very circumspect when recording her life, and Julia Briggs later called her own biography *A Woman of Passion* for definite reasons. As readers will discover in this lively concise account, Edith was indeed passionate, a Bohemian woman who led a highly unconventional life. She flouted all the social and moral rules of her time with delight. She had inappropriate affairs, wore daring clothes, and lost her temper spectacularly. She was a mass of contradictions: a feminist who didn't believe in votes for women; an extremely casual mother who still brought up her husband's illegitimate children as her own; a preposterously lavish hostess who served bread and cheese and lentils for supper with style when her money ran out.

She wrote ground-breaking, delightful books that highly influenced the children's literature of the twentieth century, yet she ached to be known as a poet. She had every reason to be outraged by her husband's behaviour yet she remained devoted. She earned the nickname of Duchess because of her grand airs and yet she was a loving respectful wife to her second husband, a jolly cockney sparrow. She was timid and fearful as a little girl, but grew into a woman of immense courage.

Elisabeth Galvin gives us a full picture of this interesting, complex woman and includes interviews with authors influenced by her work, actors who starred in Nesbit adaptations, and even an expert at Liberty's, the London emporium where Edith once bought her flowing artistic robes.

When children ask me who inspired me to become a writer I generally say it was Edith Nesbit. I joke a little, and say we both like to have buns for tea when we sell a story, we share a love of Liberty's, and we both have arms clanking with silver jewellery. I love Edith and when you've read this lively biography of her I think you will too – but I find her inspiring because of her books, not her personal appearance or her flamboyant private life.

I discovered *The Railway Children* first when I was very young, only six years old. My parents bought an eleven-inch television, a major purchase in 1951. I watched *Children's Hour* with interest but I only became totally involved when they showed an eight-part serial of *The Railway Children* (many years before the iconic Jenny Agutter film). I absolutely loved this serial and watched every episode spellbound. This was a world away from *Muffin the Mule*, the most popular programme at this time. The adaptation seemed so real and exciting and funny that I believed in this tiny black and white world showing in the corner of our sitting room and counted Bobbie and Peter and Phyllis as my best friends.

I had recently joined the children's library and chose the book of *The Railway Children* to take home. Some of the terminology seemed a little strange at first but the children themselves still seemed astonishingly real, and there were so many wonderful extra parts of the story that weren't included in the television serial. I'm sure children today still race through the book, even though steam railways are now mostly a thing of the past.

I returned again and again to the 'N' shelf in the Children's Library. I read *Five Children and It,* the story of five siblings, Robert, Anthea, Cyril, Jane and their little brother nicknamed The Lamb – and the sand-fairy Psammead, who can grant wishes. He's not the usual magic fairy, all smiles and tinsel. He's ancient, irritable, pedantic and full of pride – which makes the scene where he climbs on Anthea's lap for a warming cuddle especially moving.

It's a book about magic, of the most realistic, often uncomfortable kind, and there are two equally original and exciting sequels *The Story of the Amulet* and *The Phoenix and the Carpet*. I knew Edith occasionally 'borrowed' ideas from other authors, like F. Anstey with his book *The Brass Bottle*, so I hoped her shade wouldn't mind when I borrowed the Psammead himself, digging him up in a sandpit in the twenty-first century so that four of my own characters could experience his magic wishes in *Four Children and It*.

Perhaps my absolute favourite Edith Nesbit book is *The Story of the Treasure Seekers*. I love the playful way the story is told, with Oswald the eldest Bastable child telling the story, trying to make the reader guess which member of the family is the narrator – but on the second page is unable to resist saying:

> 'It was Oswald who first thought of looking for treasure. Oswald often thinks of very interesting things. And directly he thought

of it he did not keep it to himself, as some boys would have done, but he told the others.'

The Bastable siblings are some of the most realistic children in fiction. As Noel Streatfeild suggests in her own book about Edith Nesbit, *Magic and the Magician:*

> 'One way of gauging the aliveness of a family in a children's book is to ask yourself: "Would I know them, if they sat opposite to me in a bus?"'

She goes on to describe this imaginary encounter with the Bastables and proves her premise magnificently.

Edith has been championed by many writers, some of them surprising examples. J.B. Priestly was fulsome in his appreciation, his favourite Nesbit being *The Enchanted Castle.* Gore Vidal preferred *The House of Arden* and *Harding's Luck*, saying that Edith was 'able to create a world of magic and inverted logic that was entirely her own', complimenting her on her 'witty and intelligent prose style'. Noël Coward had loved Edith's books passionately as a small boy, sought her out as a young man, and stayed loyally attached all his life. He was reading a Nesbit children's book on his deathbed and said that 'even after half a century I still get so much pleasure from them. Her writing is so light and unforced, her humour is so sure and her narrative quality so strong that the stories, which I know backwards, rivet me as much now as they did when I was a little boy.'

The books certainly rivet me too – and I hope Elisabeth Galvin's biography will introduce many more readers to her children's books.

Chapter 1

Once Upon a Time

'They've killed him': Edith's husband Hubert Bland, when he held his son Fabian in his arms for the final time.

The death of her child is something from which a mother cannot ever fully recover, especially if she believes it is her fault. When she was 42, Edith Nesbit's life changed forever when her beloved son Fabian didn't wake up from the general anaesthetic he was given for a routine operation. On Thursday 18 October 1900, 15-year-old Fabian died after, it is believed, inhaling his own vomit as a result of eating breakfast on the morning of an operation to remove his adenoids. Edith never forgave herself for forgetting she shouldn't have fed her son within 24 hours of his procedure.

But this tragedy turned out to be the moment that altered the course of her career, turning her into one of the most well-known children's authors of all time. Fabian's death triggered something deep within Edith to express her grief in writing, the result of which is some of the finest children's literature ever published. In the seven years after Fabian died, she wrote an extraordinary nine bestselling novels. These included *Five Children and It* and *The Railway Children*.

Ironically, although writing about and for children made her famous, she always felt disappointed that she was best known for her children's fiction. She wanted to be a poet. The stories she wrote are about happy children but, sadly, none of her own children grew up to be happy adults.

Edith Nesbit was a good-looking woman with a magnetic personality that captivated most people who ever met her – she had hundreds of friends and acquaintances of all ages in different parts of the world. She was tall with bewitching hazel eyes and dark curly hair cut in a scandalously short style. She was graceful and gallant, an androgynous bohemian whose loyalty, generosity and zest for life endeared her to both men and women right up until she died in 1924. We only know all this through a limited number of letters and recollections of Edith's friends and family. She didn't write a diary and burnt all her childhood writing except for a single collection of memories. Biographers must read between the lines of her published works (which number more than 100) to discover what this enigmatic woman was really like. In one sense, Edith was a female 'Peter Pan' who never quite grew up and this personality trait turned out to be her greatest – and most unique – asset. Her life story is as rich as even her wildest imagination could have conjured up.

So, assuming you're sitting comfortably, shall we begin?

Once upon a time, on 15 August 1858, a baby was born and her name was Edith Nesbit. (She would later delight in sharing the date of her birth with Napoleon and Julius Caesar.) Her mother, Sarah, gave birth at home, which was 38, Lower Kennington Lane in London, just south of the River Thames and near the Oval cricket ground. Edith's father was John Collis Nesbit and she was the youngest of six children. There were two rambunctious, boisterous boys, Henry (nicknamed Harry, who was two years older) and Alfred (born four years before Edith). Edith had two sisters, the sickly Mary (Minnie, seven years her senior) and Saretta (fifteen when Edith was born and who would become her favourite sister). Saretta was their half-sister, as their mother was a widow. Their brother, John, died when he was only six. He had been Sarah and John's first child together and their loss cruelly foreshadowed the same devastating heartbreak Edith would eventually experience.

Lower Kennington Lane doesn't exist now, it is buried deep beneath a busy main road and giant supermarkets, but in the mid-1850s it was semi-rural farming land. The Nesbits lived on three acres, which John Nesbit ran as a small agricultural college. His unusual specialty was agricultural chemistry and he was a pioneering researcher of how artificial fertiliser improves crops.

Edith described her first home in her 1913 non-fiction book *Wings and the Child or The Building of Magic Cities*:

> 'It was in Kennington, that house – and it had a big garden and a meadow and a cottage and a laundry, stables and cow-house and pig-styes, elm-trees and vines, tiger lilies and flags in the garden, and chrysanthemums that smelt like earth and hyacinths that smelt like heaven.'

The family was respectable middle-class with notable ancestry. Edith's grandfather, Anthony (born in Northumberland in 1778) was a headmaster and successful writer of popular school textbooks. He was the founder of the college in Lower Kennington Lane, originally setting it up as a Classical, Commercial and Scientific Academy. Highly rational, he probably wouldn't have approved of his granddaughter's novels had he lived to read them, as ironically he wrote in his book on grammar *Introduction to English Parsing* (1817):

> 'Beware of reading tales and novels, for they generally exhibit pictures that never had any existence, except in the airy imaginations of the brain.'

Edith's grandmother was called Mary Collis, also of respectable heritage – she was descended from a surgeon in Sweden called Jacob Planta who belonged to the Moravian Brethren; later, Edith would be educated for a short time at a Moravian school. Anthony clearly passed his intelligence onto his three sons – his eldest, also called Anthony, became an analytical chemist; Edward was a teacher who emigrated to Australia (where Edith's brother, Harry, would eventually move to); and to John, Edith's father, the cleverest of the three. John was smart in matters of the heart as well as his career, and chose his wife well. He married Sarah Green (née Alderton) in December 1850, the daughter of Henry Alderton of Hastings, and she was kind, affectionate and intelligent. Self-effacing, shy and yielding, she spent some time in France but mostly lived in Kent and London, just as her daughter, Edith, would.

One of Edith's earliest memories was being christened when she was a toddler. As the vicar held her over the font and began the baptism, Edith took off her tiny leather shoes and threw them into the holy water pretending they were boats. Little did the priest or any of her friends and family guess how far the little girl's imagination would take her. Edith's pet name was Daisy, and another of her early childhood recollections is when she was 'planted' in the garden like a real flower. When she was three or four, Edith was dressed in her best white frock (complete with lots of frilly petticoats) for a tea party her mother was hosting. Harry and Alfred dug a hole in the soil next to the gooseberry bush and promptly squashed their clean little sister into it. From then on, Edith was one of them, a tomboy who loved climbing trees, running, swimming and making mischief. She never forgot her mucky initiation into a boy's world and years later it made her a bestselling author when she wrote about it in *The Story of the Treasure Seekers* (1899).

Edith and her brothers were cloaked in the love of their father and mother. John was an unusually hands-on Victorian dad, who played dressing-up with his children and would romp around the house with them. Sarah felt great tenderness towards her youngest daughter and Edith always treasured the first letter she ever received from her mother, whom she nicknamed 'the old mother owl' because she wore glasses. It expresses the sweet bond of love between them, a bond that Edith would never forget and often wrote about in her fiction:

'My Pretty Little Daisy,
'How kind of you my darling to help to send me a nice Handf [perhaps handkerchief?]. I shall be so glad to have you down in my bed and hug and kiss you for it.

'I shall soon be home now and I shall bring you a Baby doll which I have bought for you. It has blue Eyes and flaxen hair and is dressed like a little baby in long clothes with a white Costume Hood and Cloak. You will be so pleased with it. Mama longs to bring it home to her darling little Daisy.

'Mama hopes her little pet's cold is gone. Nurse must take great care of you and Alf this cold weather. Good night my dear little girl. Papa and Mama send you lots of love and kisses.'

Edith and her brothers shared the nursery at the top of their house in Kennington Lane, and she describes it as:

'a big room with a pillar in the middle to support the roof. "The post," we called it: it was excellent for playing mulberry bush, or for being martyrs at. The skipping rope did to bind the martyrs to the stake.'

They had a large rocking horse, a big doll's house, a Noah's Ark, a lovely tea set, a chest full of wooden bricks, and, more unusually for children today, a pestle and mortar. An animal lover throughout her life, Edith's favourite toy was a black-and-white-spotted china rabbit that she had bought for a penny at a fair. She played with him in the bath and took him to bed with her for as many as eight years. She, like all of us, was heartbroken when her favourite comforter got lost. Edith also had a rag doll; she remembers its face regularly fading and being drawn on again by her nanny:

'She was stuffed with hair, and was washed once a fortnight, after which nurse put in her features again with a quill pen, and consoled me for any change in her expression by explaining she was "growing up".'

It was while playing with her dolls that Edith came up with her first-ever heroine. She didn't love dolls as toys but saw them as characters to make up stories about. She remembers the very moment she locked eyes with her favourite one, called Renée, who had brown eyes, pink cheeks, a blue silk dress and a white bonnet decorated with orange blossoms: 'the most beautiful person in the world', she called her. Renée even had interchangeable hair that could alter from blond to brown. She came to Edith in a lucky way:

> 'I looked and longed, and longed and looked, and then suddenly in a moment one of the great good fortunes of my life happened on me. The beautiful doll was put up to be raffled, and my sister won her. I trembled with joy as she and her wardrobe were put into my hands. I took her home. I dressed and undressed her twenty times a day. I made her play the part of heroine in all my favourite stories. I told her fairy-tales and took her to bed with me at night for company, but I never loved her. I have never been able to love a doll in my life.'

This odd detachment became a personality trait that followed Edith into adulthood. Her friends knew her as a warm-hearted person who would always help those who needed it. She ignored social class status and wasn't afraid to get her hands dirty with gardening, charity work and manual labour. Yet her nickname was Duchess because of her formal, grand ways. One friend described her as the sort of women whom people couldn't feel tender about. After she married, Edith loved her husband yet was unemotional enough to accept his pathological unfaithfulness. Equally, she loved her children and adored her grandchild although would only kiss her eldest son on the forehead in a stately sort of way. In a similar fashion, she held her young fans at arm's length although it was important to her that she answered every letter and she enjoyed making friends with them. Perhaps her coldness stemmed from an awful tragedy. Very sadly, when Edith was only three, her father died unexpectedly. Only 43 years old, John was visiting a friend's house in Barnes, southwest London, on 30 March in 1862 when a lingering illness turned serious and he passed away. His obituary in the *Illustrated London News* showed he was a lively and interesting teacher who had inspired many:

> 'He delighted to gather students round him and stir up their enthusiasm for a science which he loved so well, and the high positions which many of them have since attained prove that as teacher, as well as lecturer and author, he has not laboured in vain.'

He was laid to rest in the catacombs at West Norwood Cemetery. Edith felt the loss of her father so deeply that she never got over it. It influenced the man she married, her relationship with her husband and her feelings towards other men. She constantly wrote about absent fathers and mothers in her books, most powerfully in the climax of the famous lines of *The Railway Children:*

> '"Oh! My Daddy, my Daddy!" That scream went like a knife into the heart of everyone in the train, and people put their heads out of the window to see a pale man with lips set in a thin close line, and a little girl clinging to him with arms and legs, while his arms went tightly around her.'

It must have been so sad for Edith to write these words knowing that her own father could never return; Edith looked to her mother for comfort and they were always close. Sarah was gentle, kind, loving and would do anything for her children. Helped by two nursery nurses as was customary at the time for middle-class families, she survived as a single parent and continued to run her deceased husband's agricultural college for several years. She did all she could to give her children everything they needed for a happy, secure childhood – just as Edith would describe years later in *The Railway Children:*

> 'These… lucky children always had everything they needed: pretty clothes, good fires, a lovely nursery with heaps of toys, and a Mother Goose wallpaper…'

But in 1866 the Nesbit family was to change forever, just like the family in *The Railway Children:*

> 'You will think that they ought to have been very happy. And so they were, but they did not know how happy till the pretty life in the Red Villa was over and done with, and they had to live a very different life indeed.
>   'The dreadful change came quite suddenly.'

Chapter 2

Of Brighton and Bordeaux

Edith's peripatetic childhood across France.

THE EXTRAORDINARY LIFE OF E. NESBIT

'I was a child as other children... my memories are their memories, as my hopes were their hopes, my dreams their dreams, my fears their fears.'

Edith Nesbit, *Long Ago When I was Young*

A great horn boomed through the mists of Southampton, signalling that the paddle steamer was about to leave the Royal Pier for France. A small girl stood on deck, only ten years old and travelling alone. Edith Nesbit waved a gay goodbye to the English coast and began her journey across the Channel. She couldn't wait to see her mother and sisters after weeks of being apart and smiled to herself as she imagined how it would feel to be in the arms of her loved ones at last.

It wasn't the first time Edith had been to France. Her middle sister, Mary, was suffering from consumption (tuberculosis) and had been living there for two years after the doctor advised that a warmer climate would help her recover. Mrs Nesbit had moved there in 1866 with Saretta when Edith was just seven, bravely bearing the separation from her youngest daughter and two sons Alfred and Harry by sending them to boarding school. Edith was pushed unhappily through a series of schools, and sent to live with various families in-between – friends if she was lucky, strangers if she wasn't. It must have been very unsettling and Edith later wrote:

'It is a mistake to suppose that children are naturally fond of change. They love what they know. In strange places they suffer violently from home-sickness, even when their loved nurse or mother is with them. They want to get back to the house they know, the toys they know, the books they know.'

The only period of Edith's life that she documented explicitly were these years of her childhood. A series of twelve episodes were published in the *Girl's Own Paper* from October 1896 to September 1897 when she was 38, as an established children's writer with a family of her own. It was later published as a collection, known as *Long Ago When I Was Young*.

Childhood is often recalled as a hazy wash of memories, with snapshots of big days such as Christmas and birthdays mixed in with smaller, more ordinary incidents such the taste of a favourite lunch, the shape of a mother's hands, the smell of the school classroom. But for Edith, her memory of being young remained crystal clear throughout her life and she made her career out of it. In *Long Ago When I was Young*, she doesn't always remember exact details or the names of whom she encountered but this makes her recollections all the more real as she evocatively recalls incidents, smells, colours and feelings. Some of the reminiscences seem inauthentic to today's readers; her howling distress of not being able to do maths, for example. Many children feel nervous on the day of a mental arithmetic test, but the majority probably wouldn't spend weeks crying themselves to sleep about it as Edith supposedly did. At other times in the book, some of the quoted prose is extraordinarily eloquent for a child. Nevertheless, for those who are interested in Edith, it's a useful document for several reasons – to be read as a piece of her early prose, to catch a glimpse of her young personality and as a record of what went on in her childhood. *Long Ago When I Was Young* can also be read on different levels – by an adult, a child or a parent reading to a child:

> 'Not because my childhood was different from that of others, not because I have anything strange to relate, anything new to tell, are these words written. For the other reason rather ... that I was a child as other children, that my memories are their memories, as my hopes were their hopes, my dreams their dreams, my fears their fears ... I open the book of memory to tear out some pages for you others.'

In her introduction, Edith Nesbit sets herself up as the voice of the 'everychild', claiming her experience of youth is universal. In fact, her childhood was anything but universal – she had attended five schools by the time she was ten and lived in France, Germany and Spain with no permanent home between the ages of seven and twelve. But it is the smaller, everyday experiences she had as a child – and her reactions to those experiences – that are commonly shared. They are the classic themes of any popular children's story – bullying, being scared of the dark, the whims of adults, food, hiding secrets, baths, boredom, friendship, summer holidays, the disappointment of reality, toys and games. Her anecdotes are fleshed out with comments that reinforce their authenticity, putting into words the memories that many of us have floating vaguely in our heads but can't necessarily articulate.

The first chapter indicates that Edith's childhood was desperately unhappy – although the final episode suggests it was a blissful, golden time. Perhaps this reveals Edith's tendency for the melodramatic (which became an entrenched personality trait) and is also evidence that as for many of us, childhood is a baffling mixture of highs and lows. Her first experience of school was when she was seven as a weekly boarder at Mrs Arthur's in Brighton. She was bullied and hated it:

> 'When I was a little child I used to pray fervently, tearfully, that when I should be grown up I might never forget what I thought and felt and suffered then. Let these pages speak for me, and bear witness that I have not forgotten.'

Edith's nasty year was cut short when she caught measles and she was sent to the countryside of Buckinghamshire for the summer holidays with her brothers. Alfred very sweetly gave her a real white rabbit and a hutch he had made, and the family, together again, feasted on wholesome treats from the garden – eggs laid by the chickens, fresh raspberries and honey from the comb. All holidays must come to an end, but it was a shock for Edith to attend a new boarding school for the autumn term, this time in Stamford, Lincolnshire; 'I think I should have preferred a penal settlement,' she wrote. She was constantly punished and made to go without meals for minor offences such as having dirty hands. Edith felt ugly compared with the other girls, envying the gorgeous shiny curls of her classmates and bemoaning her own unruly brown hair (even as an adult she would get frustrated about how thin and wild it was). Wanting to be beautiful is something many little (and not so little) girls can identify with and Edith used her childhood wish for beauty in her 1902 novel *Five Children and It* when the children wish to be as beautiful as the day. Edith was comforted in her Stamford boarding school with familiar objects, and it is testament to her respect for children that she sympathises with the significance young people place on their toys and tiny treasures. 'The small material objects that surround one's daily life have always influenced me deeply,' she writes. 'So large a part of a child's life is made up of little familiar playthings and objects.' In one episode, she sweetly recalls her school mug, mauve-spotted with a crack near the handle.

Edith always had a close relationship with her gentle and tender mother. She hated being separated from her so when Sarah visited Stamford and it was time to say goodbye, Edith couldn't control her emotions. 'I clung about her neck, and with such insistence implored her not to leave me,' Edith wrote. It is somewhat ironic that, as a 38-year-old mother writing about that very incident, her own children were being kept busy downstairs away from their mother. For most of her children's youth it was the housekeeper, Alice Hoatson, who largely did the day-to-day childcare. In the end, Sarah decided not to send Edith away again but instead made arrangements for her to travel in September 1867 for winter in France: 'What delicious thrills of anticipation and excitement as I packed my doll's clothes on the eve of our journey!' wrote

Edith of her European adventure, which was to take her over the course of six years across south and central France to Dieppe, Rouen, Paris, Tours, Poitiers, Angoulême, Bordeaux, Arcachon and Pau at the bottom of the west Pyrenees. After a holiday in Paris, Edith, Mary and Sarah travelled 360 miles south to stay in Bordeaux and it was here that Edith had one of the most frightening experiences of her childhood. It had such a deep impact, it would turn her into a writer of ghost stories as an adult.

Edith had always had a taste for the gruesome – in London she loved scaring herself silly by visiting the life-size stone dinosaurs at Crystal Palace, the waxworks at Madame Tussaud's and the Egyptian mummies at the British Museum; the latter would later inspire her to write about ancient Egypt in the final in the trilogy of *Five Children and It, The Story of the Amulet.* Now in France, she begged to be taken to see a collection of mummies in a church crypt and was so excited she wore her best blue silk frock. But this French display was rather more gruesome than she was used to because it was of natural mummies, rather than embalmed ones. There were about 200 grisly bodies strung up on the walls and knee-deep in hundreds of loose human bones – not a suitable sight for little girls (especially impressionable ones), as she recounts:

> '…flesh hardened on their bones… their long dry hair hanging on each side of their brown faces, where the skin in drying had drawn itself back from their gleaming teeth and empty eye-sockets. Skeletons draped in mouldering shreds of shrouds and grave-clothes, their lean fingers still clothed with dry skin, seemed to reach out towards me… On the wall near the door I saw the dried up body of a little child hung up by its hair.'

Edith was so scared that she couldn't talk about it and that night back in the hotel restaurant she thought she saw a mummy behind the curtain and jumped straight into the arms of a friendly waiter. 'The mummies of Bordeaux were the crowning horror of my childish life,' wrote Edith. 'It is to them, I think, more than to any other thing, that I owe nights and nights of anguish and horror, long years of bitterest fear and dread. All the other fears could have been effaced, but the shock of that sight branded it on my brain, and I never forgot it.' The French mummies later appeared in her book *The Enchanted Castle* (1907) as the gothic Ugly Wuglies along with the Crystal Palace dinosaurs. Edith had always been somewhat dramatic:

> 'The first thing I remember that frightened me was running into my father's dressing-room and finding him playing at wild beasts

with my brothers. He wore his great fur travelling coat inside out, and his roars were completely convincing. I was borne away screaming, and dreamed of wild beasts for many a long night afterwards.'

Edith's wild imagination made her highly strung and easily spooked when she played with her brothers and sisters. For one play, Edith had to pretend to be a princess orphan who was stolen by her sister Saretta, acting as a gypsy. When her big moment came, Edith was so shocked to see Saretta wearing a big black bonnet and ugly mask she screamed herself into hysterics and had to stay in bed for several days until she calmed down. She never forgot that mask and became scared of the dark ('my mortal terror') until she was an adult:

'One used to lie awake in the silence, listening, listening to the pad-pad of one's heart, straining one's ears to make sure that it was not the pad-pad of something else, something unspeakable creeping towards one out of the horrible, dense dark. One used to lie quite, quite still, I remember listening, listening.'

The supernatural fascinated Edith and she believed in every known superstition: she was horrified if knives were crossed over at the table, for example. It was only when she had children of her own that Edith cured herself of her fear of the dark so she wouldn't pass it on to them.

After Bordeaux, the family chased the sun and fresh mountain air towards the Pyrénées and settled in November 1867 in a *pension* in Pau, a popular resort for English visitors during the winter. Sarah Nesbit was concerned her youngest daughter was lacking in education and so packed Edith off to a local French family, where she rapidly grasped the language in just three months and became inseparable from their daughter, Marguerite, described as 'the typical good child of the French story-books. She wore her hair in a little yellow plait down her back'. Coincidentally, in French, Marguerite means 'Daisy', Edith's childhood nickname. Being settled in one place for a significant length of time did Edith the world of good, and she cried when she left and was sent to yet another new place, Bagnères-de-Bigorre. Edith screwed up her courage to make the most of another new home and was delighted with her bedroom in their pretty cottage, which was built on an arched bridge over the mountain stream – the stuff of fairytales. Dreaming of princesses, Edith loved it when her sister Saretta would sit with her and read fairytales. These would eventually be some of the first books Edith published as she re-wrote classic stories such as *Jack and the Beanstalk*. One day, Saretta wanted to make her little sister's dream come true by showing her a real shepherdess – although she didn't quite match up to the fabled character with satin skirts and a hat with roses:

> 'I stood gazing sadly at a wrinkled-faced old woman in a blue woollen petticoat and coarse linen apron... her crook was a common wooden one with a bit of iron at the end, and not a ribbon nor a flower on it.'

Poor Edith! Yet she was determined not to let the episode disappoint her and as an adult always tried to see the magic in everyday life – a personality trait that was to serve her well during countless hard times.

Christmas 1867 for the Nesbits was in Biarritz where it was warmer, and then on to Spain to hunt the sun – the plan was to spend time in San Sebastian and Irun – but Sarah Nesbit was so disgusted by the hygiene of the inns that she marched the girls right back across the border. Edith was dispatched back to Britain to live with family friends while this unexpected change of arrangements was made. Here at last she found a school she could settle in. A 'Select Boarding School for Young Ladies' run by Miss Macbean, a woman Edith described as 'one of the best and kindest women who ever lived'. 'If I could have been happy at any school I should have been happy there,' wrote Edith. Proof of this is that she stayed in touch with Miss Macbean and visited her some ten years later. In England, Edith stayed in a 'strange house in Sutherland Gardens', possibly in Kent. Her old fears of the dark crept back in the night as she wrote about one of the most frightening nights of her childhood, where she imagined there was something hiding behind her enormous four-poster bed. Edith was allowed to keep the gas light on fully but in the night, someone turned it down:

> 'I awoke in a faint light, and presently sat up in bed to see where it came from, and this is what I saw. A corpse laid out under white draperies, and at its foot a skeleton with luminous skull and outstretched bony arm. I knew, somewhere far away and deep down, my reason knew that the dead body was a white dress laid on a long ottoman, that the skull was an opal globe of the gas and the arm the pipe of the gas-bracket, but that was not reason's hour. Imagination held sway, and her poor little victim, who was ten years old then, and ought to have known better, sat up in bed hour after hour, with the shadowy void behind her.'

The next day, Edith left for France alone. She must've been a tough ten-year-old to travel on her own from England by train and boat to the French coast where her mother met her and took her to Dinan in Brittany. Sarah had rented a whole house for the summer of 1868 until November 1869. Her brothers came over from boarding school and the La Haye farmhouse became one of Edith's favourite homes, although it was reputed to be haunted with a mysterious clatter at night in the yard. When Edith and her brothers went exploring they came across a crumbling chateaux; as they looked through the boarded-up door, the straw on the floor seemed to rise up and spin itself into a rope and the children ran screaming for their lives. For the most part, the summer holiday was the stuff of wholesome adventure that would inspire many of Edith's children's novels – picnics, parties, pirates and pony rides – such delights observed by children's authors from Enid Blyton to Arthur Ransome. Edith's 1901 novel, *The Would-Be-Goods,* drew on her memories of this time when the Nesbit children gathered waste-paper baskets full of cherries that grew in the garden, alongside peaches, apricots, nectarines, and grapes. They hid in the hay loft, dug out a cave and discovered their own private stream:

> 'We built dams and bridges… we caught fish with butterfly nets
> in the sandy shadows; we called it the Nile and pretended there
> were crocodiles in it.'

Stealing provisions from the kitchen, her brothers trusted Edith to embark on an exciting adventure along the stream, almost reaching Paris (in their minds) before emerging through a tunnel back onto their front lawn:

> 'The swamp had coated us with black mud almost from head to
> foot, and in this condition we marched gaily into the garden where
> my mother was entertaining a company of rather smart friends to
> tea. The sequel was bed.'

Edith used this type of dry humour often in her novels, when the adventures, no matter how thrilling or frightening, always end up safely at home.

After the happy summer, the boys went back to boarding school in England and Edith was sent to yet another establishment – this time, one run by a Mademoiselle Fauchet. She was so homesick she ran away before the term had even started and was then introduced to the Ursuline convent in Dinan. She stayed for about a year, until November 1869. Finally, she had found her place and people; 'I was so happy there'. In a letter to her mother she writes, 'The nuns are all very kind to me though I have been very naughty.' She asks her mother if she can convert to Catholicism – something she eventually did as an adult. The nuns were probably quite shocked at the tomboy antics of their headstrong charge but were kind and gentle. Mère Marie Madeleine described Edith as 'the mad English girl, capable of anything but a good child'. One of the letters the Mother Superior wrote home to Mrs Nesbit was to tell her that Edith had been drunk!

> 'I regret that Edith should have taken wine; I believe this has been the cause of her tempers. It was her brother who brought it to her and the little girl wished to drink some of it.'

Edith held up her time on the farm at La Haye as an example of exactly what children long for; a freedom that was unusual for a child of the Victorian age. 'My mother, with a wisdom for which I shall thank her all my days, allowed us to run wild,' she wrote. Being bored is one of the greatest sufferances of being a child, according to *Long Ago When I Was Young*:

> 'A part of the infinite charm of those days lies in the fact that we were never bored, and children are bored much more often and much more deeply than their elders suppose.'

The theme of escaping into fantasy as the ultimate cure for boredom is a constant theme in Edith's novels. The endless summer holiday of the family in *Five Children and It* is enlivened when they meet the Psammead. In *The Railway Children*, the family's suburban existence is changed forever when the family move next to a steam train '…you used to say it was so dull, nothing happening, like in books. Now something *has* happened,' Phyllis says to Bobbie in *The Railway Children*.

Wishing for something to happen was a recurring feeling for Edith, who mischievously made up her own fun if none other were to be had. Once, when she was staying with a family friend who was a doctor, she mixed up the contents of his medicine bottles and put the lids back on for devilment. She was wracked with guilt afterwards – that is, until she was bored again, when she wrote to her mother about how boring it was there and the lady of the house read it and sent her home in disgrace.

Although Edith hated boredom, neither did she enjoy the constant change of scenery that characterised her childhood. After La Haye, the family left France for Germany, where Edith and her brothers were sent to school to learn an additional language. Edith ran away from her miserable Moravian school near Düsseldorf, apparently jumping out of a window to escape, but her stomach got the better of her and she had to return when she could find nothing to eat except raw pumpkin. Not much is recorded about this period of her childhood, although we know she was sent home, alone, at the outbreak of the Franco-German War in 1870. Apparently, her ship to Southampton was stranded in fog for three days and she had nothing to do but read the ship's timetables, given to her by the sailors.

While Edith had been at school, Sarah had taken the opportunity to bring Mary back to Britain for a short time. Now her daughter was 18, Mrs Nesbit was keen that she should be introduced to London's potential suitors. Mary was attracted to creative people and began mixing in Pre-Raphaelite circles where she met the artist and socialist William Morris, and the poets Christina Rossetti, Algernon Charles Swinburne – and a lesser-known poet who was blind, Philip Bourke Marston. Philip fell deeply in love with Mary, and wrote more than 50 love sonnets for her. Early in 1871, they became engaged. This impossibly romantic connection would have thrilled the young Edith and gave her a taste for the literary life in London that she would eventually become part of. Yet the love story was never to come true. Like a heroine from the fairytales Edith loved so much, her beloved sister Mary died in Normandy on 30 November 1871. She was just 19. A few years before, Edith had written a sonnet for her sister, and it must have provided some comfort to the family after the lovely young girl was taken too soon. Published towards the end of Edith's life in *When I was a Girl*, John O'London's Weekly, 15 November 1919, it is a remarkable piece of work by a 13-year-old:

> To my Sister's Portrait
> It is so lovely! Yet that portrait shews
> But one half of her beauty, auburn hair
> Falls o'er her shoulders and her throat, small fair
> Soft hands, and a delicate Grecian nose!
> Those eyes, those wells of truth and love and light
> Speak volumes to a colder heart than mine
> They are as tranquil those blue eyes of thine
> As summer sea beneath a moonlit night.
> They cherry lips make happy slaves of those
> Who hear thee speak through them their *Christian* name.
> Some love thee sadly without hope of love
> Some give thee love while hoping for the same.
> Some love thee with a love that cannot die
> And, Maris Stella, such a one am I

Tearfully, early in 1872 when Edith was 14, Mrs Nesbit and her two girls returned home along with the body of their dear Mary. They buried her with her father in the catacombs of Woolwich Cemetery; her coffin was decorated with fleur-de-lis to commemorate her death in France.

Suffering in grief, the Nesbits' fortune was to change, at least for a little time. Forever practical, Sarah had found a home for her family in the quintessentially English hamlet of Halstead in the middle of the Kent countryside, some twenty miles from London. In old English, 'halstead' means 'refuge' and this is what the family found at a time when they most needed it, after years of unsettled travelling in strange lands. Halstead Hall lay opposite a field where ponies lazily grazed; it was a pretty red-brick house built in the Regency style with white-framed sash and bay windows and roses and ivy curling around the door. The large back garden was laid to a smooth lawn, framed with chestnut trees and shrubs. Over the wall peeped chocolate-box cottages, two pubs and, in the distance, the sound of church bells. It was a rural paradise for the young Nesbits. When her brothers were home for the holidays from boarding school, they treated Edith as a tomboy, and fought with her, climbed trees with her and taught her how to swim and play cricket. It's highly probable they would have all gone on adventures along the local railway track, which lay beyond the field at the back of the garden. It ran into a tunnel with steep cuttings – just as Edith would describe more than thirty years later in *The Railway Children*.

The Nesbits were warmly welcomed into the rural community, particularly by the local rector and his young family and Edith was allowed to wander at will into their library and borrow whichever books took her fancy. Now 14, she was more or less past the accepted age of formal education. With her brothers away at boarding school and her sister Saretta living up north, Edith had hours to herself each day. She started reading voraciously and it was during this peaceful, settled, golden time that she developed a lifelong love of literature that set a path for her future career. Day by day she steadily accumulated a deep knowledge of Shakespeare and nineteenth century novels that would be forever imprinted on her impressionable teenage mind, devouring Charles Dickens, the Brontës, Jane Austen, Mrs Molesworth, George Eliot and William Makepeace Thackery. She never forgot those words she read; as an adult, one of her many party tricks was asking her family and friends to open a Dickens book and read out a few sentences: Edith was able to pinpoint the context and character with apparently 100 per cent success. As she lay in her hammock slung between laburnum trees in the corner of the back lawn, breathing in the scent of the jasmine that covered the side of Halstead Hall, Edith gulped down her favourite action-adventure tales of *Waverley* and *Rob Roy* by Sir Walter Scott and was in pure heaven. After reading all day, she would retreat to her bedroom and attempt to write her own masterpieces. For the first time she had her own room (complete with a lock to keep pesky brothers out), which overlooked peonies, currant bushes, apricots and a little pond. 'My bookcase stood by this window, an old mahogany bookcase with a deep top drawer that let down to form a writing-table,' wrote Edith as an adult, remembering her favourite childhood home. 'Here I used to sit and write verse, verse, always verse… Here I wrote and dreamed…' When Edith was 15, her mother helped her show her work to a publisher, Mr Japp, the editor of the popular Victorian periodicals *Good Words* and the *Sunday Magazine*. He was the first professional to read Edith Nesbit and he instantly knew she was something special. 'I shall never forget the rapture of delight and gratitude with which I received the news that my verses had been accepted,' wrote Edith. 'By-and-by they were printed, and I got a cheque for a guinea – a whole guinea, think of it!'

Unfortunately, a poem cannot be found under her name in either publication that year. Perhaps it was published anonymously as was reasonably common in those days. Either way, the earliest published piece under Edith's name (well, D for her nickname 'Daisy' Nesbit at least) appeared a year later in December 1876 in *Good Words* called 'A Year Ago'. She asked her mother to help her write a covering letter to the editor and, as an adult recalled this incident with the wry humour of experience:

'She dictated a suitable exercise in propriety and I wrote it out very fair. But I thought it cold and unconvincing. So I wrote at the end "P.S – Do, please, take this!". He did, too. I was seventeen then. "Please do!" seemed to me so much more sincere and sensible than "Dear Sir, I beg to enclose, etc." Perhaps it was. But when seventeen says "Please do!" they do – don't they? Later on one learns to say "Dear sir," with no passionate postscripts.'

A Year Ago

'A year ago we walked the woods
A year ago today;
The lanes were sweet with black-thorn bloom
The hedges white with May…

This year, oh love, no things are changed,
As bright a sunset glows;
Again we walk the wild wet woods
Again the blue-bell blows.

Only – our drifted spirits fail
Spring's secret springs to touch;
For now you do not care for me
And I love you too much.'

From the magical moment of seeing her name in print, Edith was hooked on writing, and it was a skill that was about to save her life.

Chapter 3

Falling in Love

Love in June
'And the summer sighed her name
as she and the sunshine came:
O sun and blue sky and delight!
O eyes and lips of my queen!
What was done there or said
No one will ever know'

Lays and Legends by E. Nesbit, Longmans,
Green & Co (1886)

The 17-year-old Edith was squashed miserably in the hollow of the roof of Halstead Hall, spooning illicit chunks of tinned pineapple into her mouth. Sighing sadly, she knew there was one last thing she must to do before she left her beloved home forever. Climbing up onto the triangular area of the roof that was hidden by gables, she carefully etched her initials into the leadwork. Reluctantly, she lowered herself back into her bedroom. As she slipped through the trap-door in the ceiling for the final time, Edith smiled as she thought about the years of secrets she'd shared with her brothers up there. She could remember their delight when they first discovered the hiding place and how they'd filled it with books and midnight feasts. With another sigh, Edith traipsed downstairs to join her mother and the mountain of packing crates that were destined for 6, Mount Pleasant, Barnsbury Square, Islington in north London.

Edith lived at Halstead Hall with her mother and brothers from spring 1872 until autumn 1875 when the Nesbits abruptly and mysteriously moved house. It is believed that Mrs Nesbit found herself in impecunious circumstances after her elder son, Alfred, frittered away the family funds. It was a disappointing and unsettling time as the Nesbits were once again homeless and temporarily lived with Edith's older half-sister Saretta at her new home near Manchester. But Edith, being Edith, found a positive in the midst of a dark situation and while in the northern city, made firm friends with a young woman the same age as her. Ada Breakell would turn out to be Edith's longest and dearest friend – and, almost, her sister-in-law. The pair giggled together as they went roller-skating at the local rink, swapping gossip about boys and books. When Edith moved to London with her mother, the two exchanged addresses and it is through her correspondence with Ada that we are able to trace one of the most significant moments in Edith's life.

When she was 19, Edith became engaged to a bank clerk; without a father, Edith was keen for a stable male figure in her life. In 1877, Ada came to London to stay with Edith and the pair visited the bank where Mr Stuart Smith worked for a clandestine lunchtime date. Standing tall in her long skirt with leg-of-mutton blouse tightly belted to show off her tiny waist, Edith was a quintessential Victorian beauty. Her shiny chestnut hair was prettily pinned up, escaping in tendrils at her neck. Holding hands with Ada, the pair swept into the bank hoping for a glimpse of Mr Smith on the pretence of changing a note. Instead they were stopped dead in their tracks by a tall, dark and handsome stranger looking them up and down with an amused expression. Mr Smith introduced them to his colleague, Hubert Bland, and unknowingly altered the course of his young fiancée's life forever. If only the young bank clerk could have been sensible of the subsequent results of his politeness, he may not have been quite so chivalrous.

With her head full of the Brontës and Jane Austen, Edith was a hopeless romantic. Hubert was three years older than her at 22 – standing taller than six feet and more than 12 stone with a thick moustache and prominent eyebrows. He had a forceful personality, a wicked sense of humour and a powerful sex drive. They fell in love at first sight. Edith immediately broke off her understanding with Stuart Smith and in a flurry of passion accepted Hubert's proposal of marriage. As Edith excitedly introduced him to her mother, Mrs Nesbit couldn't help but think her daughter was acting hastily. Sarah was suspicious of Hubert's overt confidence and affected style of dress complete with silver-rimmed monocle on a watered silk ribbon and silver-topped walking cane. She also thought his voice was somewhat strange, as it was unusually high-pitched for a man. As Mrs Nesbit was a mild and gentle soul she wouldn't dream of meddling in the affairs of her headstrong daughter, yet she made it plain to Edith that Hubert was not suitable marriage material. Edith, however, wouldn't listen – she couldn't, she was head-over-heels in love.

During the weeks that followed, Edith and Hubert snatched every moment they could to be together, meeting illicitly during his lunch break at the library of the Guildhall off Cheapside. They talked for hours about literature and politics and found a shared passion in the topic of social injustice. At the weekends the couple wandered through the countryside hand in hand. Once Edith took him by train back to her beloved Halstead Hall and she described the romantic liaison to her friend Ada by letter, in feminine, pretty handwriting:

> 'Yesterday was awfully pleasant. Mr Bland and I went to Halstead and had no end of a "nice time" – we went into the woods – and sat about – caught (and kissed) a chaffinch – …the most charming day I have ever spent. The country was fresh, young and jolly. So were we…'

Years later, Edith wrote a short story called *A Holiday* about a young poet and a teacher who meet on a train and get off at Halstead together. They fall in love over a picnic and talk about the romantic poets Keats, Shelley and Browning. Edith Nesbit's previous biographer, Julia Briggs, in her excellent and thorough work *A Woman of Passion*, put two and two together and pointed out that Edith was really writing about her own life in that story, and that this quote is about how Edith fell in love with Hubert that afternoon:

> 'And to the end of her days no one will ever know her soul as he knew it that day, and no one ever knew better than she that aspect of his soul which he chose that day to represent as its permanent form.'

Hubert Bland was a devastating seducer. He had fallen in love for the first time at eight years old, began smoking cigars by nine and lost his virginity at 12. Women swooned over him and men couldn't help but admire him, this tall and commanding Victorian gentleman who oozed confidence in his stiff collar and white cuffs, dark hair parted in the middle. Under his formal black frock coat, Hubert's body was muscular from swimming, athletics and boxing. Yet behind his impressive demeanour was hidden a humble cockney from East London. Mrs Nesbit had been absolutely right not to trust him.

Born on 3 January 1855 to Henry (a commercial clerk) and Mary Bland of 22, Wood Street in Woolwich, Hubert was the fourth child after Henry, Percy and Helen. His grandfather had been a plumber and painter (on his father's side) and a publican (on his mother's). As G.E. French points out in *Hubert Bland: A Personal View* (published by The Edith Nesbit Society, 2006), from a young boy, Hubert was a social climber, one of those people who is determined to live a different life from the one they were born into. He believed that the class system was necessary for a successful state but that didn't stop him trying to traverse it. Hubert used his brains to work hard in class, with the motivation of getting his ticket out of Woolwich through the army. On his way to school, he would stand on Woolwich Common and watch the blue-coated officers parading past from the Royal Military Academy, Kitchener's former training ground. Hubert was mesmerised by the horse artillery and was inspired by the sound of the bugles; he would listen out for the blasts from the Woolwich Arsenal testing grounds sounding across the Plumstead marshes. But when he was 11 years old, he was forced to discard all thoughts of such aspiration. His father died suddenly, leaving his family in a precarious situation. After grieving for her husband, Hubert's mother gently broke the news to her son that there would be no money to pay for his commission into the army. Although greatly disappointed, Hubert kept his chin up and made the most of his situation – just as Edith had done at a similar age when circumstances forced her to travel through unfamiliar France with her ill sister. Hubert finished school as best he could and got a job with the civil service. When it didn't suit him very well, he found work as a bank clerk and in his spare time got his military fix through the Artists Volunteer Corps. Hubert's other hobby was politics although his passionate beliefs were somewhat in conflict – he was a sort of a Tory socialist. Although fiercely patriotic, he was a great supporter of Woolwich's regular social protests because he believed the majority of working men weren't benefitting from Britain's vast Empire.

By the time he reached 22 years old, Hubert was a man in the prime of his life and determined to make a difference to the world; it all added up to a package that was completely irresistible to Edith. As they celebrated their first Christmas together, Edith gave him a gift of a small, leather-covered notebook inscribed with the words, 'To Hubert Bland from Daisy Nesbit, for Xmas 1878' and copied into it one of the most famous love poems ever written, 'How do I love thee? Let me count the ways…' from *Sonnets from the Portuguese* by Elizabeth Barrett Browning. Their love affair became more and more passionate until the summer of the following year when Edith turned 21 years old and Hubert gave her the ultimate gift; himself. Sex before marriage was unheard of amongst nice middle-class young ladies but Edith's attraction to her fiancé was so strong she threw social convention to the wind and enjoyed herself with abandon. Finally, three years after they met, Hubert made an honest woman out of her when they married on 22 April 1880 at the City Register Office.

The Easter daffodils were turning yellow bringing cheer to London after winter and as Edith walked to the church she should have felt happier than she ever had done before. She was marrying the love of her life, a handsome, clever and admired man who utterly adored her. Yet the day she had dreamed of was sadly unromantic. The only guests at the wedding were two strangers who acted as witnesses. No photographs, congratulatory greetings cards nor diary entries survive of the occasion. We don't know whether Edith wore a wedding dress or what sort of flowers she carried, if any at all. Both Edith and Hubert wrote down false addresses on the marriage certificate and Edith doesn't give her father's full name. The mystery of Edith's sad and strange wedding is explained by a single surviving document; a birth certificate. The couple's first child, Paul Cyril Bland, was born 22 June 1880, meaning Edith would have been seven months' pregnant on her wedding day. Victorian convention would have been so shocked by this that Edith had to hide her pregnancy from absolutely everyone, including her best friend Ada (whom she asked to be godmother after the birth) and possibly even her mother. It simply would not have been possible in polite society to invite guests to a wedding of this sort. To keep her situation a secret, Edith left home during that heady summer of love with Hubert in 1879, and squirrelled herself away into confinement in a grotty bedsit away from Islington in Greenwich, at 8, Oxford Terrace, now a smart address of 16, Dartmouth Row, on the edge of Blackheath. She used a false name, Mrs Bland, to secure the lodgings but Hubert didn't live with her at first and stayed at his mother's in nearby Woolwich. Edith didn't get on with her prospective mother-in-law, which worsened the situation.

On a summer's day in London, a new baby boy was born to 21-year-old Edith. Without the support of her mother, sisters or friends she possibly laboured alone, ignorant about childbirth as the subject wasn't one that was readily shared in polite circles. But, when she held her son in her arms for the first time, Edith had never felt such a joy and it was a moment she never forgot. Edith had been blessed with a healthy child who was very much wanted by both his parents. Paul's first proper home was in Lewisham. Today, the house is marked with a blue plaque, but then number 28, Elswick Road was just an ordinary terraced house in an ordinary London suburb. For a passer-by glancing through the window, it should have been the very picture of Victorian domesticated bliss. Yet the truth was altogether different. Hubert wasn't properly living with his wife and young baby as he continued to stay for part of the week with his mother in Woolwich. He had given up working as a bank clerk and became an entrepreneur as a brush manufacturer. Quite what Edith thought of this madcap idea, we will have to speculate. Hubert was hiding something. Two things, actually. He had a secret fiancée who had given birth to a son earlier that year; Maggie Doran was the daughter of a dyer from Beckenham and Hubert's mother's paid companion. Hubert had proposed to her at about the same time as he proposed to Edith. Maggie, Edith and Mrs Bland Senior were merrily unaware of Hubert's love triangle, and the latter was dropping heavy hints that her son should take Ms Doran up the aisle sooner rather than later. Hubert would continue the affair for more than ten years until his mother died in 1893. He held his nerve for four of those years, spending several nights a week at his mother's with Maggie and the rest of the week with Edith and his son. From what we know of Edith, she was no pushover. A romantic certainly, but surely no fool yet she learned too little too late of her husband's obsession with women as the awful truth slowly and horribly dawned on her. In the linen notebook in which she first doodled her beloved's name entwined with hers during that fateful August of 1879, underneath the name Daisy Bland written in carefree cursive is darker ink and later handwriting depicting the terrible words underlined 'deeply regretted'.

Perhaps this abrupt and heart-breaking wrench from her cherished and happy childhood to a woman with a child of her own meant Edith never properly grew up. Yet whatever she felt in her heart, Edith's head told her to survive. In a display of matter-of-factness that was to become characteristic, she took a deep breath, rolled up her Victorian leg-of-mutton sleeves and got on with the job of caring for baby Paul in a strange neighbourhood almost as a single mother. Most impressively of all she found work to keep her family afloat. Edith's new name may have been Bland but this formidable woman was not going to live her new life without colour, vigour or vim.

Chapter 4

A Victorian Working Mother

To a Young Poet
'Write, write, write! Produce, produce!
Write for sale and not for use.
This is a commercial age!
Write! and fill your ledger page.
If your soul should droop and die,
Bury it with undimmed eye.
Never mind what memory says –
Soul's a thing that never pays!'

Lays and Legends by E. Nesbit, Longmans,
Green & Co (1886)

Other newlyweds in 1880 were following Mrs Beeton's advice on the best way to draw a fowl and how to fold napkins into the shape of a vase. But not Edith. Once she had made her new surroundings as cosy as she could with homemade curtains and cushions, she had more serious considerations. London was suffering a smallpox epidemic and Hubert caught it twice in the summer of 1880, shortly after their son Paul's birth. It was extremely rare to catch the disease more than once and Hubert had to live apart from Edith and Paul for two months while his mother nursed him back to health. It was probably about this time that Edith had found out Hubert's Maggie Doran-shaped secret, possibly through her habit of opening his letters. Hell hath no fury like a woman scorned but for Edith, not so much. Although her temper became legendary in later life, as a twentysomething she took the astonishing step of going to visit Maggie and making friends with her. Her gesture was genuine as the women would stay friends until Maggie died in 1903. The young Edith had begun to adopt a bohemian outlook on life – after all, she had had an unconventional upbringing without a father or permanent address. Now her husband had turned out to be unconventional, she began reconsidering the traditional notions of marriage and the role of women in society. Edith and Hubert believed themselves to be advanced thinkers and had come to the conclusion that marriage was a bourgeois convention that they weren't going to be bound by. Essentially, all that mattered was that they loved each other more deeply than anyone else and it was therefore inconsequential how many other people entered into the equation.

Life was never dull with Hubert and, once he had recovered from smallpox, a further dramatic twist resulted in his business partner disappearing along with all the company funds. It was disastrous timing because of the current economic depression, and during much of the 1880s the Blands were virtually bankrupt. Edith's loyalty to her husband was once again tested; little did she know how many times it would be challenged throughout their marriage. Faced with demands for rent and bills, Edith was forced to spend economically and replaced the traditional red-meat diet of the day with cheaper eggs, risotto, rice, home-grown vegetables, macaroni, well-stewed chicken, lentils and beans. With a baby son and an unemployed husband, Edith was forced to become the family breadwinner and it would be a struggle that continued for an entire decade. Her mother, Sarah, lived with them, presumably to offer a much-needed hand to Edith.

Nice middle-class girls didn't work and certainly not if they had started a family but Edith had no choice. She had never had a job in her life but she turned to what she knew; writing. Late every night she would stay awake in front of the fire, forcing herself to dream up romantic tales of Victorian love affairs, sentimentally sweet animals and adventurous boys and girls to submit as short stories to the many magazines on the market. She wrote for both adults and children and composed poetry, too. Sometimes with a tablespoon of gin mixed with water to keep her going she would sit at the table, writing neatly and steadily in her feminine loopy handwriting. Few crossings-out spoilt the thin squares of blue and green paper that she threw down onto the floor after they were filled with words. When she was writing notes on plot or character, she would use both sides of the paper, and for work to be submitted to an editor she wrote on only one. She scribbled notes on the top of the paper to sum-up the mood of the writing such as 'calm, ordinary'. When Edith's mind wandered she would doodle and work out sums in the margin. On nights when the work was pressing, she wrote 'URGENT' at the top to motivate her. When her eyes stung and her head began to ache too much to write any more, she gathered up all her work and carefully numbered each page before blowing out the candle and falling into bed, exhausted. In the morning she woke with fresh enthusiasm to sell her stories, and would kiss her son goodbye and catch the train from Lewisham to Charing Cross. In the 1880s, London was a dark, grey place of fog and gas light; a noisy city with clattering horses' hooves on the cobbled roads. Edith carried her stories in a brown paper parcel wrapped up with string and made her way down Fleet Street past the famous flickering Bovril sign and dodging the hansom cabs, conscientiously visiting every office on her long list of editors. It was tough work, repeatedly untying that parcel to show what she'd written – there were scores of writers competing for commissions. By October, she had sold just two poems to the *Sporting Times*. Years later she wrote about the experience in *The Railway Children*, when the character of Mother is forced to keep her family afloat by writing stories:

> 'Mother, all this time, was very busy with her writing. She used to send off a good many long blue envelopes with stories in them – and large envelopes of different sizes and colours used to come to her. Sometimes she would sigh when she opened them and say, "Another story come home to roost. O dear, O dear!" and then the children would be very sorry.
>
> 'But sometimes she would wave the envelope in the air and say: "Hooray, hooray. Here's a sensible Editor. He's taken my story..." Whenever an Editor was sensible, there were buns for tea.'

Edith made it all sound quite romantic but the reality was gritty. Forget buns for tea, what the Blands needed was bread on the table. Edith had to constantly come up with new ideas for stories and not miss a single deadline. She wrote, '...it is uphill work – writing when you don't feel a bit inclined... What seems to be the worst of my present life is that I have no time to do any good work – in the way of writing verse I mean...' Edith always had aspirations to be a poet, and loved the work of Tennyson, Browning and Swinburne. But this wasn't a time to indulge in creative writing; a year later Edith was pregnant again and desperate for a regular stream of income. The craze for hand-painted greetings cards was in full swing and she began painting Valentine and Christmas notelets selling them directly to printers in London. She only got a few pence for each one but they were much-needed regular commissions. Edith used small brushes and coloured paints to depict pretty forget-me-nots, yellow daisies, violets and cherry blossoms before composing verses for the inside. For an extra-special touch, she would add real pressed ferns. Once she was two days late with a batch of Christmas cards and was distraught when the printer refused to take them. Exhausted from nights of staying up late with pregnancy hormones running high, Edith burst into tears. Taking pity on her, the printer changed his mind and paid her after all.

Every penny counted for the Bland family when another hungry mouth to feed appeared on 2 December 1881. Mary Iris was a sister for Paul and the little girl was named after Edith's beloved late sister and her grandmother, Hubert's mother. She would be known as Iris, and, adored as she was, there was no opportunity for Edith to enjoy the Victorian equivalent of a baby shower nor maternity leave. From day one she had to juggle her domestic duties with writing and, fortunately, she had enormous energy to do so. How's this for an impressive load on a Sunday? Edith wrote to her friend Ada:

> 'I have done two sheets "sides into middle" [cutting sheets in half and sewing them up the middle to make them last longer] – written some paragraphs for a newspaper – cooked the dinner, nursed Iris for a whole hour – in the vain hope of getting her to sleep… I eventually gave up. – I have also painted some cards… I do hope the supply will now be kept up…'

Just six weeks after Iris' birth Edith was back on Fleet Street, literally hungry for work. It was on one freezing lunchtime in January 1882 that Edith's fortunes changed when she met someone who would be deeply significant in her – and Hubert's – life. Her name was Alice Hoatson. Like a ghost among the gas lights, Edith was in the city trudging up yet another staircase to show yet another editor yet another story. She was cold, hungry and miserable as she knocked on an office door. A Yorkshire voice asked her to come in and Edith walked into the room to see a woman about the same age as her squatting on the floor at the gas stove making some cocoa. Kindly, the woman asked her to sit down and offered her a cup. Edith gratefully gulped it down and with tears in her eyes, accepted a sandwich. Shivering and shaking with cold, Edith asked the woman if she would consider having a look at a story she'd written. The Yorkshire lass introduced herself as a journalist for *Sylvia's Home Journal* and promised to take a look. She was busy on deadline but said Edith could warm herself up by the stove before she left. They said goodbye and at 5pm Alice finished work and on the train on the way home to Brixton where she lived with her widowed mother, she read Edith's story. She loved it.

Arriving at work the next morning, Alice was keen to get the story printed promptly so that the poor wretched writer could be paid as quickly as possible. But when she got to the office at 10am, she saw the same thin, pale, ill-looking woman waiting for her at the door. Edith asked if she could swap the piece for a different one as her original story had been accepted for another magazine.

Alice agreed without even reading the new feature. She knew this woman needed help. Thus, the die was cast for Alice and Edith's long, dramatic and ultimately self-destructive friendship. Alice later described this first meeting as 'the tie that held us for the rest of her life'.

An extrovert, Edith gleaned her energy from others and always loved making new friends. Alice and Edith had plenty in common and Edith repeatedly suggested that her friend 'chuck' her badly-paid job so they could work together. Edith asked Alice to move in with them, and when Alice said she couldn't leave her mother behind in Brixton, Edith considered inviting the mother as well. 'She fell in love with all my family,' wrote Alice, 'and would insist that she knew we were of the same stock as herself…' Alice would often stay the night at Elswick Road when Hubert was away at his mother's during the week. Edith and Alice would work together into the night, painting cards fuelled by gin mixed with water. 'The pay was small and the labour light but we were glad to get anything,' said Alice, who would later describe Edith as, 'My dearest friend, companion in work and play during our young womanhood and up to the last four years of her life.' Alice was a cheerful, capable soul who listened sympathetically to Edith while rolling her sleeves up and helping with the housework and looking after the children. Although Edith was genuinely keen to be friends with Alice, it also suited her to have the domestic help so she could concentrate on writing. Although they had plenty in common, Edith was an extrovert and Alice the introvert who was happy to stay in the background. Edith was keen for Alice to meet her husband and he, in turn, was intrigued with stories of his wife's new friend. Finally, Alice and Hubert were introduced in May 1882 when she was fatefully brought into the Bland's social circle. Alice wasn't prepared for how handsome he was, despite his smallpox-marked cheeks. Hubert liked what he saw, eyeing up this petite brunette before pressing his hand in hers to shake it.

Hubert was back in work and feeling powerful, looking every inch the smart Victorian office man, complete with tall silk hat, rolled umbrella and morning newspaper. He was earning a decent wage as a secretary to a hydraulic power company and as he travelled into London by train with the masses each day, he was determined not to get swallowed up into insignificance. He was firmly resolved to make a difference to the world and began to hone his skills as a journalist by helping Edith with her writing. She didn't always enjoy her commercial magazine stories so he would sometimes finish them off or think of new ideas. His favourite topic was politics and eventually they began writing together under the name Fabian Bland, their work appearing in publications such as London' radical newspaper *Weekly Dispatch*. By 1884, they were 'going shares' in all the stories that Edith was commissioned. 'I am sure it is much better when we write together than when we write separately,' Edith wrote to her friend Ada Breakell in April that year. The husband-and-wife-team would write together until the late 1880s, when Edith concentrated on her children's novels and Hubert became successful in his own right as a political journalist. One short story earned them £10, two months' pay for workmen of the time. Throughout her life, Edith believed in luck and it was such superstition that helped keep her going as a freelance writer. She drew her own lucky sign, a four-leaf-clover that was made up from her and Hubert's initials, and it began to work. She became famous among editors for never turning down a job and constantly worked hard to write anything she could for magazines, illustrated booklets and pictures that were sent to her. Slowly, her fortunes changed. Her poems and short stories for adults and children started appearing with increasing regularity in a wider variety of magazines such as *Belgravia, The Weekly Dispatch, The Argosy* and *Longman's Magazine*.

Edith and Hubert eventually found time for creative writing and in 1885 when Edith was 27 years old they published their first novel together under the name Fabian Bland, *The Prophet's Mantle*, based on the real story of the Russian revolutionary, Peter Kropotkin and his time in London. Kropotkin would eventually become friends with the Blands, along with another Russian exile, Stepniak, who would appear in the plot of *The Railway Children*. Edith and Hubert were delighted with the success of *The Prophet's Mantle*, published by Henry Drane and reissued twice, and Hubert began a tradition for his wife by buying her a silver bangle for every novel she published. *The Prophet's Mantle* is largely forgotten today but it remains significant because it strangely foretells a dramatic incident that would rock the Blands and Alice Hoatson to the core. The heroine is called Alice Hatfield who becomes pregnant by her socialist lover. It was a prophecy that was about to come true.

Chapter 5

Edith's Transformation

'I have something dreadful to break to you gently... I have Cut my hair off!!!!!!!'

Letter from Edith to her friend Ada Breakell in 1885

British women in the 1960s went braless to make a political statement but Edith Nesbit had beaten them to it in the previous century. In her mid-twenties, Edith represented the equivalent of the swinging sixties woman when she cut off her hair, wore frocks without corsets, took up smoking and joined a political movement. She started reciting her poems in Working Men's Clubs and met people she'd never have otherwise come across – whose radical ideas changed her view of the world and forever influenced her writing. Smoking was unusual amongst women but it was a habit Edith adopted until late on in her life, and one that became her trademark. She got into the habit of having the first puff of Hubert's cigar and she'd roll her own cigarettes, twenty-five at a time, extremely quickly without looking at what she was doing. Absent-mindedly, she constantly burnt holes in her clothes and would forever be embroidering over the burns. The long cigarette holder dangling from her lips became as much an accessory as her scarves and jangling bangles, and she always carried a long box containing her tobacco – sometimes, for the shock factor, in a corset box. Nothing was more scandalous than having short hair, though, and Edith was brave enough for the chop. 'I have something dreadful to break to you gently... I have Cut my hair off!!!!!!! I retain the fringe – but at the back it is short like a boy's. I wonder how you will like it. – It is deliciously comfortable,' she wrote to her friend, Ada. A dramatic change of hairstyle is sometimes a metaphor for a significant change in a woman's life, and Edith was undergoing a transformation. Dissatisfied with the ugly effects of the Industrial Revolution, she and Hubert became interested in the Aesthetic Movement, a romantic, bohemian outlook that hoped to change society's view of female beauty and inspired people to look for beauty in everyday life. Two of its most famous figures were Oscar Wilde and Dante Gabriel Rossetti, the brother of the poet Christina Rossetti whom Edith greatly admired. Together, Edith and Hubert retreated into the thirteenth century, reading poems by Swinburne and gazing at paintings by Burne-Jones. 'We tried to live the life of a more lovely age,' wrote Hubert, '…a world of strange beauty and bizarre romanticism; a rocco world wherein brave gentlemen wore glittering armour and fair ladies dressed indescribably.' Taking inspiration from medieval damsels, Edith took to wearing woollen clothing in colours of the past; soft, clinging gowns of old gold, silver grey and sage green. She dressed her four-year-old daughter Iris in loose pinafores and, later, Persian bedspreads, much to the girl's embarrassment.

Edith dared to make a social statement by what she wore (or didn't wear) and, although she wasn't interested in fashion, her style of clothing became as much her trademark as her style of writing. Edith once wrote, 'I never wished to change the outward appearance or rather the selfness of my body with all its defects.' Scandalously, she threw away her corset and favoured flowing silk dresses of the aesthetic style made famous by the London department store Liberty from 1884 until the mid-1920s. Underneath she would have probably worn just a slip. 'She was quite brave not to wear a corset. It was quite rebellious,' says Anna Buruma, the head of archiving at Liberty London, who explains that the phrase 'Liberty gown' was used as a generic term at that time to describe a flowing dress of a certain style. Designers would use the word 'Liberty' to mean 'quality'. 'Liberty gowns at the time were completely the opposite of corsets,' says Buruma. 'They were worn by artists and those with pretentions to be artists. These people rejected the notion of Parisian fashion and were proud to ignore trends and wear something that lasted for a long time.'

Although she liked to look dignified and would be constantly irritated by her thin, messy hair, Edith dismissed fashion and berated women for their interest in it:

> 'The knowledge that the question of dress will not be one to be almost weekly settled tends to calm the nerves and consolidate the character…I wish I could persuade women to buy good gowns and grow fond of them… and to refrain from the orgy of the fancy shop. So much of life, of thought, of energy, is taken up with the continual change of dress…. Such a constant twittering of nerves goes on about all those things which don't matter.'

With wafting scarves and bangles jangling up her arm, Edith's unusual dress was often written about by her friends and contemporaries; the novelist

Berta Ruck described her as, 'a tall handsome richly-coloured woman in an unfashionably waistless green Liberty robe, hand-embroidered at yoke and cuffs…' For most of her life Edith wore almost all of her clothes in the same style and made many of her own garments. She loved putting five or ten pounds in her pocket and hunting for remnants at Henry Glave's haberdashers on New Oxford Street. She wore dark blue or dark brown when she was younger, and brown, dim green or a dark maroon as she got older. Her eccentric outfits included an Indian bedspread made into a gown and a jacket that she called 'a coat of a thousand ears' made from musquash ears. Alice Hoatson would often embroider Edith's dresses for her.

Although she didn't care for fashion, Edith did care about appearing graceful and always followed her motto to live beautifully according to the Aesthetic ideal. She was conscious that her manners, movements, voice and clothes were always arranged gallantly and pleasingly – and even when she grew old and overweight people regularly remarked how charming she looked. She was never clumsy, walked slowly and was careful to choose clothes that flattered her figure. At the height of her literary success she had a screen by the door of every room in her house, which she used to hide behind to arrange the long train of her dress before she walked in so she always looked the part. Some people thought this was a rather affected way to live. To others, she didn't quite succeed. One of her colleagues described Edith as, 'one of those very flustered ladies. Her clothes never seemed quite right, and she was always losing scarves and things.' He recalls the noise of her jangling accessories, '…those beads and bangles and incessant cigarettes'!

Edith compiled a short story about an advanced woman, called *Miss Lorrimore's Career* (1894) and it appeared in *The Yellow Book*, a sort of bible for aesthetic writers. William Morris was a follower of the Aesthetic Movement and was a key figure in the Arts and Crafts Movement. Although better known today for his wallpaper and stationery designs, Morris was a leading social activist of his time. As an influential thinker, designer and writer during the 1880s, he persuaded the great British public that art should be made useful and enjoyed at all levels. He championed the ideals of hard work, craftsmanship, and the quality and natural beauty of materials. When writing her poetry, Edith was heavily influenced by his ideas of the past and distrust of machinery; she loved the countryside and wanted to protect it above everything. Edith and Hubert met William Morris through the Fabian Society, the socialist group that the couple had become part of, from which the modern-day Labour Party has its roots. Through the Society the couple was expanding their circle of friends in London.

Hubert had always been interested in socialism, and the boom-and-bust years following the Industrial Revolution had made it difficult for him – along with many others – to find a job. Britain suffered high unemployment, poverty, urban squalor and poor living and working conditions with aristocratic land-owners dominating government. During the Great Depression of 1873 to 1896, a surge of socialist parties and literary societies were formed as people like Hubert joined together in mass numbers to discuss how to achieve a better future. He once wrote:

> 'I can never remember a time when I looked upon the world around me and saw it was good... to our stupefied minds and stricken spirits politics seemed to lose their value.'

Described today as Britain's oldest political think-tank, the Fabian Society was officially formed in January 1884 and Hubert chaired the first meeting, with Edith as a fellow founding member. The Society's aim was to achieve a fairer Britain in a peaceful way. From this moment on, Hubert dedicated his life to the pursuit of a better country. He was an unusual Fabian because he also held deeply conservative opinions such as imperialism and was against women being allowed to vote. His private morals may have been shabby and his outward appearance of a gentleman a sham but his commitment to the Fabian Society was a genuine attempt at improving the lot of the masses. He once wrote:

> 'Before all things [socialism] would mean the wider freedom of the Many... and in many cases even abolish, the legal and personal privileges of the Few.'

Today, the Fabian Society remains at the core of Britain's Labour Party beliefs. The Society was formed at 17, Osnaburgh Street in London's Regent's Park. Hubert was elected to the executive committee and served as treasurer, a position he held until 1911. The Society wanted to establish a democratic socialist state; Britain in the early 1880s was the most industrialised nation in the world and also its most powerful with an Empire that spanned a sixth of the Earth's surface. But rapid industrialisation had meant unprecedented urbanisation with half of Britain's population living in cities, causing housing, education and healthcare problems. Unlike Karl Marx, the founder of communism, Fabians didn't advocate a revolution but rather worked towards a fairer society through peaceful and gradual change using the power of local government and trade unions.

EDITH'S TRANSFORMATION

The most prolific left-wing movers and shakers of the time followed the movement. Hubert invited George Bernard Shaw to join the group – and others included H.G. Wells, Eleanor Marx (Karl's daughter) and suffragettes Emmeline Pankhurst and Charlotte Wilson. Other prominent left-wing figures included Sydney Olivier, Graham Wallas, Annie Besant and Beatrice and Sidney Webb, the couple who argued for a national minimum wage and a welfare state. Hubert brought Edith into the Society, and she was described by one member as 'the most attractive and vivacious woman of our own circle and would appear prominent at our meetings'. In March 1884, Edith was elected onto the Pamphlets Committee to write socialist literature. Her first, *Why Are the Many Poor?* would become famous. Edith was thrilled and shocked that she had been given this influential responsibility. 'Now can you really fancy me on a committee? I surprise myself sometimes,' she wrote to Ada Breakell. 'Personally, I don't think much of [the pamphlet] – but you can't expect a working man's style to be much, and his facts are all right.' As the Fabians grew into a larger group that met in public places rather than private homes, Edith became less interested in going to meetings although she always held the principles of the Fabian in her heart and in her writing. 'Work is the only noble thing,' she once wrote.

Edith's many letters to Ada around the year 1884 provide a fascinating insight into Edith's social and physical transformation. Ada had moved to Australia and Edith missed her terribly, so she shared lots of detail of her life back home in London so that her friend wouldn't forget her. Edith left her two young children at home with the hired help and began socialising in the evenings at debates, readings and meetings through the Fabian Society and other groups such as the Lewisham Literary Society, Hampstead Historical Club (also known as the Karl Marx Society), the Browning Society and the Shelley Society:

> 'We felt we had had the misfortune to be born in a stupid, vulgar, grimy age, an age, too, that was getting stupider, grimier, more vulgar every day ... we turned away from it to a little world within a world, a world of poetry, of pictures, of music, of old romance, of strangely designed wall-papers, and of sad-coloured velveteen.'

Edith was introduced to people she probably never would have come across and heard ideas that might not have occurred to her before – she called her new friends 'human warriors' and wrote to Ada of her intellectual transformation:

> 'How different I was this time last year! – Now I see the world through "larger, other eyes" – but the increased light brings with it infinitely increased sorrow.'

She discusses whether she has it in her to be a truly great person:

> 'I wonder if it is hard to be great. It seems to me that all our lives
> we are trying not to be great – I fancy the real obstacle to human
> greatness lies in the backyardness of the human mind to conceive
> it. Greatness is around us on all sides, but we are mistrustful
> of the fact, and while its sun shines in upon us at every instant,
> we are forever shading it off with our timid hands. Greatness is
> easy – not difficult.'

Edith began reading widely, from the teachings of a German utopian to radical
suggestions of equality between the sexes. She wrote to Ada:

> 'The Fabian Society takes up a good deal of my thoughts just
> now. I am also doing a good bit of serious reading – Among
> other things, Büchner's Man, Mill's Subjection of Women, Louis
> Blanc's Historical Revelations and an intensely interesting book
> which Harry [Ada's sweetheart and Edith's brother] would like
> called Esoteric Buddhism by Sinnett. You see my reading is rather
> mixed and miscellaneous – but it is the fate of most women only
> to be able get a smattering, and I seem to want to read all sorts of
> things at once.'

She writes enthusiastically of the beliefs of the Fabian Society:

> 'Its aim is to improve the social system – or rather to spread
> its news as to the possible improvement of the said S.S. [social
> system]. There are about thirty members – some of whom are
> working men. We meet once a fortnight – and then someone reads
> a paper and we all talk about it.'

She mentions a new acquaintance, a painter and decorator. 'I like him so much.
There are "all sorts" in the F.' Edith talks about people from different walks of
society, of varying ages, both men and women – from 'clever spiritualists' to
'youthful idealists with large heads'.

'Don't you think these sound as if they would make an interesting society
well-mixed,' she asks Ada. She tells of a new couple she enjoys spending time
with because, 'The talk is always talk, not frivvle – and withal, they are not prigs.'
However, Edith shows she doesn't take it all too seriously when she interrupts her
political discussion with an eccentric story about her awful toothache.

In another letter of around the same time she proves herself a witty pen-pal and goes on to share the goings on in her life, a mix of serious news and domestic gossip:

> 'I happened to find this sheet of paper and it looked inviting... We are going out a good bit just now to all sorts of places and meeting all sorts and conditions of men. Sometimes I enjoy myself and sometimes I don't – which is the way of the world I suppose.'

Edith goes on to describe a dress that she made from a Butterwick's pattern – joking that it doesn't suit her but she is thrilled that it fits and is pretty. 'I made it myself -! -!' she excitedly writes, describing the eccentric garment as 'terracottery crushed strawberry mixture nun's cloth with dark velvet bodice and trappings'. Edith enjoyed her body and the affect it had on Hubert and would often stretch out in front of the fire, her willowy figure displayed for his pleasure.

As well as – and perhaps as much – as the political subject matter, Edith loved the drama of the Fabian Society, as some of the brightest brains in London tried to outsmart each other in debates. Although there is no doubt that Edith believed in the Fabian ideals and hated injustice and suffering, she couldn't take the meetings or its earnest participants too seriously. She would often make a noise, pretend to faint or ask for a glass of water just to liven things up. Privately, she made rude remarks and judgements about her fellow female Fabians, which show her up as rather superficial. Fellow members criticised her for not taking the meetings seriously. But what annoyed the Fabians the most is that Edith steadfastly refused to support the cause of votes for women. It was a topic many of the female Fabians felt strongly about, such as Annie Besant, Charlotte Wilson and Emmeline Pankhurst. Edith criticised such feminists, calling them militant, unfeminine and, ultimately, psychologically disturbed. The inconsistency of her beliefs is one of the great mysteries of Edith's character. Throughout her life, she enjoyed a freedom far beyond the norm for women of the time. She wrote strong, capable female characters, both children and mothers, with fathers often somewhat ineffectual – *The Railway Children*, her most well-loved novel, is perhaps the best example of this. Edith explained her anti-suffrage stance by saying that all men should be given the vote first – at that time, only approximately 60 per cent of adult men were entitled to vote according to value of their income and land. She also said that if women were given the vote, they would only follow their husband's influence so there was no point in awarding them the right. Edith herself was easily influenced by people she liked, and Hubert was vocal in his anti-suffragette beliefs, so perhaps Edith's loyalty to her husband meant she had no choice but to agree with him. For his part, Hubert believed men and women are fundamentally different with opposing roles in society and therefore can't be treated in the same way. His standpoint was that denying this fact would disrupt progress and hold up advancing the real cause of socialism. He could be described as sexist:

> 'Woman's metier in the world – I mean, of course, civilized woman, the woman in the world as it is – is to inspire romantic passion... Romantic passion is inspired by women who wear corsets. In other words, by the women who pretend to be what they not quite are.'

Whatever the irregularity of their convictions, Edith and Hubert's lives were so passionately entrenched with the pursuit of socialism that they named her third child, born 8 January 1885, Fabian. As with Iris, pregnancy and birth couldn't diminish Edith's extraordinary energy and it was about this time that she added another string to her professional bow – reading her poems in Working Men's Clubs. She joined with a new friend, Marshall Steele, a professional public speaker who taught elocution lessons, just as Professor Henry Higgins did in *Pygmalion* (1913), written by Edith's new friend George Bernard Shaw. Performing in public would surely have given Edith great confidence – she may have been writing under the disguise of E. Nesbit but she was becoming a visible presence in public. By this time so was Hubert, whose natural tendency for argument had turned him into a respected lecturer and debater especially in Scotland and Manchester. He attracted such crowds that Manchester's *Sunday Chronicle* newspaper asked him to write regularly about social problems, and this turned into a weekly column that he would keep up until the day he died. Hubert became one of the most influential journalists of his time, persuasively and eloquently debating all sorts of issues in his 'Hubert' column, from what makes a gentleman, to the correct use of women's garters (and why Queen Victoria wore hers around her neck) to why people mustn't be bullied into having more children despite the country's declining birth rate. A good journalist's skill is to turn complicated facts into readable stories and Hubert's accessible, brotherly tone of voice encouraged everyone to become interested in issues of the day. A closet working-class hero, Hubert had found his ideal career. His years of columns reveal an opinionated man brimming with ideas, keen to debate with others of a smart mind, especially young people. His favourite saying was 'the respect due to youth' and he was popular with men but criticised by female readers who said he wrote about 'selfish pigs of men and wretched women'. In 1886, Hubert was offered the editorship of a left-wing review paper called *To-day*, with prestigious writers including the Norwegian playwright Henrik Ibsen and also George Bernard Shaw, who put him up for the position. The publication didn't make much money but was respected for its calibre of contributors.

As their professional reputation – and bank balance – grew, Edith and Hubert aspired to a larger place to live; the practice of renting rather than buying property was perfectly acceptable amongst the middle-classes, and, in fact, preferable. Some families might buy a smaller place to rent out but the generally-agreed sentiment was to delegate the bother of property maintenance to a landlord. It is estimated that around September 1884, Hubert and Edith took a lease on a large and lovely semi-detached house at 5, Cambridge Road (now Cambridge Drive) just off Eltham Road in Lee, southeast London. It was a smarter street than they were used to, surrounded by greenery and significantly grander and more spacious than their previous homes. Set over three floors with high ceilings, bright sash windows, a good-size drawing and dining room plus five bedrooms, it was the perfect family house for six-year-old Paul, five-year-old Iris and baby Fabian, who was born there.

Official records are scanty but it is thought that the Blands lived at Cambridge Road from the last quarter of 1884 until at some point in 1886, when they moved around the corner to the adjacent street, Dorville Road, and took a lease on number 8. The house was demolished in 1970, but a small children's park named after Edith Nesbit now stands nearby. Unfortunately, the Bland family's happiness was to be marred by an awful event that happened almost exactly a year after little Fabian's birth, in February 1886, which almost caused 27-year-old Edith to lose her mind. She suffered a stillbirth. The baby was a girl and Edith was so deeply distraught she wouldn't put the infant down. Alice Hoatson wrote that she spent 90 minutes trying to prise her from the tiny body so the baby could be buried in the garden:

> 'E never forgave [the doctor] for the loss of her baby…
> 'This baby I prepared for burial and E had made me promise to bring it to her while Hubert was digging its grave in the garden. I had got a long fish basket and dressed the poor mite, laid her in it and put flowers all around… then I took it to E. She had promised to let me take it away in a quarter of an hour. By that time I ought to have known the worth of her promises! Well I didn't. For one hour and a half I struggled to get it from her while Hubert came to know what had happened to keep me. At last she let him take it; he looked so wretched he could not hide his misery.'

The tender image of the perfect newborn girl surrounded by flowers is heart-breaking. After carrying a baby for nine months only to lose it at birth, Edith, who had three young children in her care, needed significant emotional support. She also needed physical help when she caught the measles shortly afterwards and so Alice Hoatson moved in with the Blands. Dressed in grey with a timid personality, she looked so small compared with the tall, robust and handsome pair of Edith and Hubert that they nicknamed her Mouse. The children would always refer to her as Auntie, and Alice described herself as a satellite to Edith's comet. 'She never relinquished her efforts to get me to join my lot with hers,' wrote Alice of Edith. 'In 1886 I gave in, being seriously ill at the time. I was on a visit to her at the time and she nursed me so tenderly through it I could resist no longer.'

But Alice wasn't seriously ill; she was unexpectedly pregnant. Unmarried, the question of whose baby it was hung in the air. But the truth was so awful that Alice couldn't bring herself to reveal it even to her best friend. For, astonishingly, the child she was carrying was Edith's husband's. Hubert was the father of Alice's baby.

Chapter 6

A Famous Liaison

'You had no right to write the preface if you were not going to write the book.'

Edith Nesbit to George Bernard Shaw

Edith stared at the art nouveau tiles around the fireplace as the flames flickered brightly. She should have been spending the evening writing but she couldn't stop thinking about Alice's unbearable situation. One of her closest friends was pregnant, unmarried and about to become a social outcast. There must be a way to help her, Edith told herself, thinking hard. And slowly, suddenly, it came to her. Alice could move in with them to live as their permanent secretary and housekeeper. The pregnancy could be kept secret if Alice stayed at home until after the birth, and when the baby was born she, Edith, would adopt it with Hubert – they could pass it off as their own in public but at home allow Alice to nurse it.

It was a clandestine plan worthy of a plot in one of Edith's novels. When Edith suggested it to Alice, who knew the truth of the situation, she guiltily refused the help. But Edith wouldn't take no for an answer and as Alice's condition grew visible she had no choice but to go into hiding with the Blands. On 19 October 1886 she was safely and secretly delivered of a daughter named Rosamund Edith some 11 miles away from home. Rosamund's birth certificate records the father was John Hamilton, a mariner, and the mother, Alice Hamilton, formerly Hoatson, living at 8, Dorville Road. The birthplace was recorded as 69, Pentonville Road in Islington, which could have been a private address although was possibly a mother's refuge. As far as we know, not a single soul other than the three of them knew a thing. Could Edith have known who the father really was? Some of her friends believed she was sensible all along and calmly confronted her close friend soon after the birth. Others, including Rosamund herself, insist Edith discovered the illicit secret six months later causing a huge row, with Hubert threatening to run away with Alice. As an adult reflecting on her unusual circumstances, Rosamund recalled that she discovered the secret of her birth when she was eighteen. Her account of events is:

> '[Edith] discovered that A.H. [Alice Hoatson] was going to have a child but she did not know who the father was and A.H. steadily refused to tell her. After the child was born she befriended A.H. and took her into her home. (Before that she had often begged A.H. to live with her altogether). And then six months later made the discovery that the father was her own husband. By this time she had grown to love the baby so much that she could not part with it. Now my father's story to me was this (and I imagine I am the only person he ever told it to). When it transpired who was the father, there was, quite naturally, the hell of a scene and I and my mother were to be ejected then and there onto the street. Whereupon my father said that if we went he went too. He said he never loved his other children as he loved me and that he was passionately in love with my mother. Finally the matter was thrashed out and the decision was taken that they should all remain together. This business recurred several times during the first years of my life. I mean, there were other occasions when A.H. was told to go and take me with her, but my father prevailed and the situation continued until it became permanent...'

A very different version comes from one of Edith's oldest friends, Helen Macklin, who was with Edith shortly after Rosamund's birth. She insisted the truth was far less dramatic. 'There was no 'discovery' but a voluntary admission of what she had long believed, made when they were specially drawn together,' wrote Helen, recalling that Edith had been seriously unwell after Rosamund's birth and Alice had looked after her:

> 'When she was recovering, she begged R.M [Rosamund's mother] to tell her the truth. (She had suspected it from the first.) She could forgive it, she told her, but she wanted it not to be denied. "I know it is Hubert, only tell me." – I well remember her words and tone and look. – Then R.M admitted it. After this Edith went into no more details: I remember not her words, but the impression I received, which was comforting and not saddening... an impression of reconciliation and peace.'

Helen Macklin argued that it would have been very uncharacteristic of Edith to banish from her home her best friend and newborn baby – although Edith's famous quick temper and sharp tongue could have given that impression in the heat of the moment:

> '…she might at some time have said in a flash what she so little meant that she never thought of it again: and to a hearer's mind it might have a different weight and emphasis. I can only guess…'

However she discovered the truth, Edith blamed herself for what had happened. 'It was my own fault,' she wrote. 'I might have prevented the opportunity. I didn't and I deserved the consequences.' Perhaps Edith recognised the irony of it all; that she was the one who had introduced Alice to Hubert and that some six years back she had found herself in exactly the same position as Alice – unmarried and pregnant with Hubert's child. A deeper connection was that just as Edith lost her baby to stillbirth, Hubert had impregnated Alice. Perhaps Hubert was attracted to Alice because of the Yorkshire woman's uncomplicated devotion to hearth and home as their housekeeper and nanny while Edith was busy writing. Hubert was convinced that the average woman didn't want to work and shouldn't have to; the male role in society is to look after women so they wouldn't have to work for a pittance in factories, fields or workhouse, or sell their bodies. If a woman is a widow or a single mother, she should be provided for by the state. 'Speaking broadly, we still hold fast to the view that woman's place is her home, that her duties are to her husband and to her children,' he once wrote.

The story has yet a further dramatic twist because Edith was not an entirely innocent party. Over the summer of that year, she had embarked upon a dangerous liaison with a man who would become one of the world's finest writers. George Bernard Shaw met Edith through the Fabian Society, which he joined on 16 May 1884 – famously written in the minutes in his handwriting is a note saying 'this meeting was made memorable by the first appearance of Bernard Shaw'. He was right: the Fabian meetings could be dry and Shaw livened them up with his sharp wit, sparkling intelligence and mischievous humour – the female members adored him and hung on to every word he said in his bewitching Irish accent. Edith, who knew him as Bernard, described him as 'irresistible' to Ada Breakell:

> 'A certain G.B. Shaw is the most interesting [member of the Fabian Society] … G.B.S has a fund of dry Irish humour that

is simply irresistible. He is a clever writer and speaker – is the grossest flatterer (of men, women and children impartially) I ever met, is horribly untrustworthy as he repeats everything he hears, and does not always stick to the facts, and is very plain like a long corpse with a dead white face – sandy sleek hair, and a loathsome small straggly beard, and yet is one of the most fascinating men I ever met.' [1]

Shaw was awarded the Nobel Prize in Literature in 1925 for his ability to convey entirely new thoughts and ideas through different sorts of mediums. His intellect was broad enough to conjure up comedies of manners such as *Pygmalion* (1913) as well as intellectual and philosophical dramas such as *Man and Superman* (1903). A vegetarian who refused alcohol, his passionate socialist beliefs saw him become a vital part of the Fabian Society, both through his power as a writer and speaker as well as because of the important new members he introduced. It was Hubert who brought Shaw to the Fabians after the men had met at the editorial offices of *The Christian Socialist* and they became great friends. Later, Shaw would give Hubert a huge leg-up in his journalism career. Shaw regularly visited the Blands at home and in his diary of 18 May 1885 he even wrote that he boxed with Hubert (perhaps in the front room?), 'Put on the gloves with Bland and had a spar,' the diary records. What's the bet that Edith was egging the two men on?

Edith and Shaw's relationship was taken to the next level when they became involved professionally. Shaw introduced Edith to a work contact, his friend and neighbour Robert Ellice Mack, an editor and publisher. Edith began writing regularly for him, both verse and children's stories, and he was a vital stepping-stone in her career and financial stability. It was in the summer of 1886 in her late twenties that Edith fell in love with Shaw. No explicit confession has ever been discovered but it is known that the pair became extremely close because Shaw revealed that Edith proposed they run away together. Julia Briggs, Edith Nesbit's previous biographer, read between the lines of George Bernard Shaw's diaries. 'A memorable evening!' he wrote on 26 June 1886:

> '...on the whole the day was devoted to Mrs Bland. We dined together, had tea together and I went out to Lee with her, and played and sang there until Bland came in from his volunteer work.' [2]

Still a struggling writer, Shaw spent all the money he had on Edith that day and bought her dinner. Ironically, he used money he had borrowed from Edith but made sure he paid her back as soon as he could, which amused her '…you still owe me something – and I suppose will remain always in my debt,' she wrote in a love letter to him. They were words that would later taunt her with cruel irony. But for the moment, the pair wandered blissfully around London; amongst the roses of Regent's Park one day, through the historical artefacts of the British Museum the next. They'd sit on the banks of the River Thames together ('pretty scene' wrote Shaw) and nibble at takeaway 'toads' (a beer-battered type of sausage) from Charing Cross station whilst discussing such subjects as whether children should be whipped. They had romantic dates in little Italian cafes, a vegetarian restaurant called the Wheatsheaf and also took tea at Shaw's flat, on the same road where the Fabian Society's meetings were held at Osanburgh Street in Regent's Park. Other times they'd take long evening train rides together.

Shaw would always see Edith safely to an omnibus or onto the train home at Charing Cross – except for the night of 8 July 1886 when, scandalously, he came back to Lee with her. He wrote in his diary that he returned home to Bloomsbury at 3.30am after a two-hour walk. Was Hubert away at his mother's that night? We shall never know what transpired between the pair that heady summer's evening – famously, Shaw had kept his virginity until a year previously and Edith might well have pushed off any of his physical advances as she was known to be a prude. Perhaps she encouraged him with a night of love that mysteriously transcended the physical. Either way, the couple were brought so close by their shared and secret satisfaction that Shaw introduced Edith to his mother two weeks later (he lived with her until he was 42). Edith was convinced the introduction was a significant step forward in their relationship, for the next morning she was so desperate to see her lover that she arrived at his flat far too early and he was still having breakfast. 'She had lost her head a little,' Shaw would write in retrospect.

An afternoon in the country would be their next date ten days later, as the pair took the train to Chislehurst, before sharing the long walk home together. '…she was very attractive. I was very fond of her and paid her all the attention I could,' Shaw wrote in his diary about his lover. As Shaw celebrated his 30th birthday on 25 July, Edith was compiling the best of her poetry for a collection to be published later that year called *Lays and Legends*. It contains many romantic poems including one called 'Love Song': did Edith write it for George Bernard Shaw?

> 'Light of my life! though far away
> My sun, you shine,
> Your radiance warms me every day

Like fire or wine.
Life of my heart! in every beat
This sad heart gives,
It owns your sovereignty complete,
By which it lives.
Heart of my soul! serene and strong,
Eyes of my sight!
Together we can do no wrong,
Apart, no right.'

But as the summer ended, their sweet affair began to sour. A notorious ladies' man, Shaw was also involved with several other women. One of his diary entries, on 20 August, shows that he enjoyed the company of no less than four on the same day. 'Mrs Bland at the Museum in the afternoon. Saw her to a bus at the corner of Chancery Lane. Gave her some tea at an Italian cafe on the way. J P [Jenny Patterson] here when I came in. Got to Wildwood Farm [Charlotte Wilson's house for a meeting of Hampstead Historic Society]. Mrs Besant there. Walked to her house with her.'

These other women included Jenny Patterson, the older widow who was one of his mother's music pupils and to whom he had lost his virginity on his 29th birthday. Mrs Charlotte Wilson was a prominent Fabian as was Mrs Annie Besant – and who was so in love with Shaw, she begged him to come and live with her. Shaw's other women included William Morris' daughter May and Karl Marx's daughter, Eleanor. By September, Shaw began making excuses not to see Edith as often and wouldn't invite her up to his flat. This diary entry records their meeting with dull formality, missing the spark and excitement of his earlier comments:

'September 15: Finished review. Worked slowly and with difficulty. Mrs Bland came to the Museum in the afternoon and would not be denied coming here to tea. Drove her to London Bridge and walked back…'

At the beginning of October, Shaw notes that he went for a long walk with Hubert in the rain – although he doesn't record what they spoke about, could they possibly have discussed Edith? Both men were known for their love of long walks. On 18 October Edith wrote to Shaw to ask him to review *Lays and Legends* for the publication she edited with Hubert, *To-Day*. But Shaw refused, saying he was too busy. Were the poems just a bit too close to the bone? He eventually wrote something about them but it wasn't very complimentary:

'If the genius of Charlotte Brontë were compounded with that
of Mrs (Barrett) Browning, and attenuated with vinegar, an
E. Nesbitt might be the result.'[3]

He describes Edith as a clever and graceful writer but says asking him to
review her work would be like pulling her teeth out. In the end, he reviewed the
collection favourably but in the *Pall Mall Gazette*, calling his review 'Found at
Last – a New Poet'. Shaw and Edith continued to socialise with each other in
the evenings, but usually in the company of other friends. It seems the frisson
between them had diminished and they had returned to being simply friends, as
Shaw's diary of 25 October shows:

> 'Wrote a batch of reviews. Mrs Bland at Museum. She lunched
> at Wheatsheaf with me and Joynes. She asked me to meet her
> at Kings Cross in the evening and go for a walk. It rained. She
> insisted on going to Enfield. I insisted on going third class for the
> sake of company…. When we got to Enfield it was very wet. I
> got her some hot whiskey to prevent her from catching cold. We
> returned first class. Got out with her at Kings Cross Underground
> and saw her to Pentonville where she was staying. Got home just
> after 1 in the morning.'

Edith came to understand that their affair was over and Shaw also reflected on
their relationship in his diary at the end of the year:

> 'Reading over my letters before destroying them rather disgusted
> me with the trifling of the last two years or so about women.'

Shaw may have been over Edith but Edith wasn't quite over him, and she
wasn't going to let their affair finish without a fight. She was hurt when
he didn't invite her to visit his new house and Shaw wrote in his diary in
March 1887:

> She insisted on coming to Fitzroy Square. My Mother was out,
> and she went away after an unpleasant scene caused by telling her
> I wished her to go, as I was afraid that a visit to me alone would
> compromise her.'

One of his much later letters recounts a quarrel they had:

'I remember a well-known poetess (now no more) saying to me, when I refused to let her commit adultery with me, "You had no right to write the preface if you were not going to write the book."' [4]

In *Lays and Legends*, Edith published a poem that seems to describe her feelings at the time and here is part of it:

'The Quarrel
…Did my heart forge the bitter words I said?
Did your heart breed those bitterer replies –
Spoken with plovers wheeling overhead
In the gray pallor of the cheerless skies?
Is it worth while to quarrel and upbraid,
Life being so little and love so great a thing?

…How dare we crush the blossom of our life?
how dare we spill love's sacramental wine?
Kiss me! Forget! We two are living now,
And life is all too short for love, my dear…'

Although they might not have kissed over it, Edith and Bernard Shaw made up and remained friends for the rest of their lives. He had become inextricably linked with the Bland family, and would later pay for the education at Cambridge of their youngest son. They influenced each other's work, both bringing out plays of similar titles (and ironic ones considering their relationship); *The Philanderer* (Shaw) and *The Philanderist* (Edith). After Edith died, Shaw wrote about their love affair, saying he found her 'a charming and attractive woman' and that he had 'tried to be attentive and kind to her'. He refused to reveal the nature of their closeness, however, and even at first declined to be interviewed by Edith Nesbit's first biographer, Doris Langley Moore, who contacted him in 1931. His secretary wrote a polite letter:

'…as Edith was an audaciously unconventional lady and Hubert
an exceedingly unfaithful husband [George Bernard Shaw] does
not see how a presentable biography is possible as yet; and he has
nothing to contribute to a mere whitewashing operation.'

Shaw was chivalrous enough to conceal any embarrassment over the Blands'
open marriage but eventually was persuaded to share some anecdotes with

Mrs Langley Moore. When she asked him if he had been in love with Edith he answered, 'No, I've never been in love with anybody – much.' He amended Langley Moore's account of their relationship:

> 'She yielded herself to the luxury of being in love. Her sentiment, which she made no attempt to disguise, elected from its object nothing of equal ardour, and was soon happily transmuted into a gay and untroubled friendship.'

Shaw asked Langley Moore to remove the words 'equal ardour' and replace them with 'but a heartlessness which he knew how to make amusing'.

It's difficult to tell whether Edith was driven by hurt over Hubert's affairs into the arms of the irresistible Bernard Shaw or whether it was her tit-for-tat attempt to get back at her unfaithful husband. Either way, she was left confused and embarrassed by Shaw's sudden withdrawal of love as he fled back to Mother. Meanwhile Hubert was quite comfortable with any adulterous thoughts his wife may have had; perhaps Edith had inadvertently validated his wish for an open marriage as he merrily continued to spend several nights a week away from the family home with Maggie Doran. For Edith, who would always crave the love of the stable father figure she had lost all those years ago, the summer of 1886 was a time when she became an adored woman again. Shaw's extraordinary mind and dazzling intellect would forever affect her writing – and her sense of self.

Chapter 7

Bohemia

'They rode bicycles in bloomers, they were absolutely unconventional and careless... Mrs Bland was a smoker of cigars at this time... she just went her own way and was the centre of a group of people who did likewise...'

Edith's neighbour

The row of houses standing along Dorville Road in Lee were identical, exactly the sort of home you'd expect in a respectable London suburb. Except for one. Bright paint bedaubed the door and porch of number 8, making it stand out from all the rest.[1] Visitors would come and go at all hours, and on Sunday afternoons a steady stream of guests dropped in throughout the day. The people who opened and closed the brightly-coloured door were different from their neighbours, too. They dressed differently for a start – in loose clothing of odd colours – and they had unusual jobs, as artists and writers. If one of the neighbours hurrying by couldn't resist a nosy glance through the front window, they would have seen plenty to gossip about. Fabians sitting next to artists, novelists chatting to journalists. The women would be wearing loose velvet dresses in green and yellow, curled up sinuously on Tate sugar crates covered with cloth and tucking in to hearty bowls of lentils, beans or suet pudding. With plenty of red wine and beer the conversation was passionate and intense.

Edith and Hubert Bland were curiosities in the conventional suburb of Lee, constantly shocking the neighbours with their unusual lifestyle that was part of an undercurrent of bohemia which was pulsating through London's veins. Edith caused a scandal when she was seen smoking and tucking her long skirts into her knickers to ride her bike. '...they were absolutely unconventional and careless,' wrote one neighbour. '...[they] were condemned and generally disliked by the very respectable neighbourhood of Lee. In fact no rumour or gossip was considered too bad to be believed about them...' People thought Edith a neglectful mother as she encouraged Paul, Iris, Rosamund and Fabian to run wild in the streets so they could taste the freedom she had so enjoyed as a child. The Blands were aloof, believing themselves to be superior in manners, taste and intelligence from their philistine neighbours. Hubert wrote of their commitment to the bohemian ideal:

'The result of this deliberate search after a sort of esoteric happiness, of this detachment from popular interests and the affairs of the workday world, of this attempt to escape from the insistent sordidness, the blatant ugliness of our surroundings, to create as it were, an interior realm of art and poetry, of rehabilitated romance, was a deep and a malign pessimism – so far an empirical, not a philosophic, pessimism, but a pessimism of conviction all the same.'

As her writing helped her become well known, Edith's circle of bright young things gathered momentum. Bernard Shaw may have dismissed her first published collection of poetry, *Lays and Legends*, but a certain Mr Oscar Wilde didn't. The epitome of the late Victorian bohemian, Wilde was impressed with Edith's poetry and wrote to tell her so:

'Dear Mrs Bland
'Thank you so much for sending me your volume of poems. I have been turning over the leaves, tasting as one tastes wine, and am fascinated by the sonnets... but I am keeping the book as a whole for study in the Clumber woods next week. You see I am getting to know you, petal by petal, but I will not touch the larger poems just now.
    'Any advice I can give you is of course at your disposal. With regard to your next volume but you do not need to be taught how to tune your many-chorded lyre, and you have already caught the ear of all lovers of poetry...
Oscar Wilde'[2]

Wilde praised her for giving 'poetic form to humanitarian dreams, and socialist aspirations', and described her as 'a very pure and perfect artist'. He called her verse 'Leaves of Life' 'remarkable' and described many of her poems as true works of art, praising her 'exquisite sense of colour', and 'delicate ear for music'. Edith was thrilled to receive his letter and struck up a friendship through correspondence with him, although they were never to meet. *Lays and Legends* sold steadily, boosting Edith's confidence tremendously. Now established in London with a strong circle of friends and having celebrated her 30th birthday in the summer, she was game enough to host a charity Christmas party. In 1888 she invited twenty underprivileged girls and boys from the nearby deprived area of Deptford to her home. There were sandwiches, cake and lemonade by the Christmas tree with singing and then each child was offered presents of a toy, a useful gift and a sweet treat. Edith continued the tradition for ten years, and it grew larger and larger as she couldn't bear to turn any child away – one Christmas a thousand turned up. The parties were held at Deptford Board School at St Hughes Fields and the event became more and more elaborate, with Edith throwing herself into it heart and soul and persuading all her friends, acquaintances and family to help. The story goes that one year everyone spent months beforehand sewing boys' blue corduroy trousers. As an extrovert who loved dressing up and showing off, Edith wrote pantomimes and held rehearsals for three months – sometimes twice a week – to get the show absolutely right. She even let her bills rack up with local shops in order to prioritise paying for the parties, 'How can I let the Deptford children starve to pay butchers, bakers, etc.!' she once said. Eventually the tradition had to come to an end when Rosamund caught scarlet fever at the party and became seriously ill. But for the rest of her life, Edith remained passionate about the injustice of the divide between rich and poor and it became a common theme in her writing. A version of her parties for the children of Deptford appears in the 1909 collection of short stories about children called *These Little Ones.*

When their lease on Dorville Road ended, the family had enough funds to move to a larger place close by; Edith was being regularly commissioned to write children's stories and Hubert was in demand as a book reviewer for the *Daily Chronicle* and for society snippets for a stock-exchange journal. The Mouse, Alice Hoatson, moved with the family, of course, and describes their new home at 2, Birch Grove as having a long, fine drawing room, a good dining room and a decent-sized kitchen. Although today the house has been replaced with a modern townhouse, the original semi-detached homes on the opposite side of the road remain so it's possible to see what sort of step-up Edith and Hubert had made in the renting ladder. It is recorded in the 1891 Census that Edith's mother, Sarah, was living with them so it must have had space for an extra adult. The new house had room for dancing and Edith would play the piano and vamp (take requests for improvised dance tunes). The mix of guests to Birch Grove was always eclectic – Bernard Shaw mingled with Hubert's lover Maggie Doran, who knew the famous socialists Sydney Olivier and Graham Wallas. Other famous names of the day such as Olive Schreiner and Annie Besant would hobnob with Cecil Chesterton and Hilaire Belloc. As many as forty people would turn up to enjoy a simple supper of herrings, cheese and bottled stout. Afterwards there would be dancing and 'always the spirit of originality, freedom and difference,' wrote one party-goer. Edith loved talking late into the night and playing games, especially drawing competitions where players would have to make up pictures from random lines. She was excellent at word games, such as Subjects and Adjectives, rhyming games and writing nonsense sentences. So successful were her informal gatherings that Edith set up a literary society, calling the group 'It' to poke fun at other, more pretentiously named gatherings. One of the members was the actor, writer and artist Laurence Housman, brother of the poet A.E. Housman. Close to Oscar Wilde and openly gay, he was friends with Edith for ten years and he stayed in touch by sending her screwball postcards he wrote and illustrated. Another famous member was E.M. Forster, known as Morgan to his friend Edith. He was still a young writer at this time; in later years his book *A Room with a View* would become one of her favourites. Forster addressed It about the Marriage Culture of Indian and Burmese Tribes, which no doubt fuelled a debate on whether the British institution of marriage was outdated. The society became infamous for its racy debates and after three years it was scandalously shut down after a talk called Nudity in Art and Life featured a description of a young woman lying naked on a tiger skin in front of the fire.

As bohemians, Edith and Hubert weren't motivated by money, and subsequently didn't manage it very well. Edith would rack up IOUs from the butcher and baker and then write madly to pay them off. During the week she would lock herself in her study at the top of the house with a 'do not disturb' notice on the door and refused to see anyone who visited her. But in 1894, the Blands scraped together the funds to move again, to a large detached house in a nearby suburb called Grove Park. The pretty Three Gables house in Baring Road lived up to its name with its distinct triple triangular gables feature, framed with chimneys, bay windows and a large, attractive driveway. Unfortunately, it has been replaced with flats (Stratfield House) although the railway is still visible from what was the back garden, and the footpath running alongside is named The Railway Children Walk. The Bland children loved playing along that stretch of railway line between Grove Park and Hither Green. They seemed to have got up to all sorts of adventures that would later inspire their mother to include in her novels, such as taking off their stockings and shoes and putting on their shabbiest clothes to sell posies they'd made from flowers in the garden to unsuspecting locals at the station. While at Grove Park, Edith got into the habit of smoking about forty cigarettes a day, despite her doctor's advice that she should limit it to twenty.

'The Blands' was a very pleasant and stimulating house to go to, and they must have been the most hospitable creatures in the County of London,' wrote Edith's friend the young novelist Edgar Jepson:

> 'It was a house of youth: they seemed to have no use for the old; they seldom encouraged the middle-aged and never the dull… though civil to their neighbours they were never intimate with them; they believed that the native residents would bore them by a lack of understanding. The native residents did not understand them; but how they did gossip about them!'

Their circle by this time had widened to Joseph Conrad and Ford Maddox Ford, and a tale of one of the parties of that time is that the housemaids danced with Hubert and guests after everyone got drunk on his 'claret cup cocktail' of red wine and Champagne, to which he forgot to add soda water. The cook was so inebriated on whisky that the bottle had to be hidden in the guest room so she wouldn't drink any more. Edith acted as a sort of mentor to Jepson, as she had begun to do with many other young writers, and enjoyed playing the role of a sexy, domineering patron in their lives. Jepson wrote:

> 'Mrs Bland… was an uncommonly clever and often amusing woman and as generous a creature as I ever came across. Not only was her purse always at the service of her hard-up friends and all the distressed who crossed her path, but there was no end to the pains she would take to get them work and straightened out their affairs and keep them on her feet. She was masterful indeed… and she rather queened it over the young writers and painters she gathered round her and directed their lives with a ruthless precision…'

Yet although highly unconventional, Edith was an odd stickler for some types of ultra-respectable standards, such as punctuality, always sitting up straight and grammar – she hated Americanisms and would always pick people up for using slang.

By this time she had struck up a friendship with the woman who regularly illustrated her stories for magazines, May Bowley, who became a frequent guest at Three Gables. Bowley recalls Edith wandering about parties with a guitar slung across her shoulders, gathering guests around the piano for a sing-song in her rich, commanding voice. She wasn't shy about tinkering on the piano too:

BOHEMIA

'Mrs Bland called me Lorelei because of my, then, very long hair. At their unconventional gatherings I was often required to let it down... [which] astonished strangers who might come into the room.... The company was of course very mixed. One young lady from the East end took Miss Hoatson aside and said 'Let's sit here and have a nice talk about the fellers.'

As the original Victorian party girl, Edith's gregarious, extrovert nature embraced bohemianism and she delighted with the new friends she made through it, both famous and otherwise. As the 1880s drew to a close, she was a part of the radical fin de siècle movement that would see in the new century.

Chapter 8

The Libertines

'No two people were ever married who were better calculated to make the worst of each other.'

George Bernard Shaw

Edith had been given a taste of love in Bernard Shaw's arms and she was hungry for more. From 1887, she began a string of affairs with young men, often poets or artists whose careers she helped advance. 'Don't you think young men are very soft as a rule?' she wrote to her friend Ada, 'and yet most of them seem to have some actual not negative good in them, which is more than we say for all our own sex.' She fell in love with the optimism of the young, and when they loved her back it proved to be a balm that would restore Edith's belief in romance. She enjoyed mothering her young gents and was extremely generous with her money and time with them, but also could be incredibly jealous. Her young lovers were all a little scared of her domineering personality and no one would dream of taking liberties with her; they'd jump to attention at Edith's command. Sometimes they found her suffocating; the story goes that one quietly escaped from her when they were on an Underground platform together.

'I was hers from that moment, and have been hers ever since,' wrote the romantic poet Richard le Gallienne, who fell in love with Edith when he saw her at a literary gathering in Hampstead. He was tall, dark and extremely handsome with large, intense eyes and gorgeously thick, wavy hair. Edith also fell passionately in love with him and even threatened to run away with him after a bad shouting match with Hubert. (Typically, it was Alice who calmed her down.) Le Gallienne's recollections of Edith after she died are tender and full of affection:

'Though it is so many years since I saw her, my remembrance of Edith Bland is as keen and beautiful as ever, and I can still see her, as though it were yesterday, as I first saw her at Hampstead, seated in an arm-chair with her two little children at her side. It was a romantic moment for me, for she was the first poet I had ever seen, and, a youth just come up to London from the provinces, I looked on her with wonder, and captivated by her beauty and the charm of her immediate sympathetic response. I fell head-over-heels in love with her in fact. She was quite unlike any other woman I have ever seen, with her tall lithe boyish-girl figure, admirably set off by her plain "Socialist" gown, with her short hair, and her large vivid eyes, curiously bird-like, and so full of intelligence, and a certain half-mocking, yet friendly, humour. She had, too, a comradely frankness of manner, which made me at once feel that I had known her all my life; like a tomboyish sister slightly older than myself. She suggested adventure, playing truant, robbing orchards and such-like boyish pranks, or even running away to sea ... At that time I would be about twenty-three, and she, I think, would be about eight years older.'

Le Gallienne was born in Liverpool and his father wanted him to become an accountant. But a love of literature proved stronger and after hearing a lecture by Oscar Wilde and failing his exams, he moved to London and became one of the original members of the Rhymers' Club with W.B. Yeats. He met Edith in 1889 as he lived near her socialist friend Charlotte Wilson and they were close for several years as she encouraged him with his work, and he remained indebted to her for the rest of his life. He found Edith's androgynous face and figure thrilling, and once gave her a book of his poems inscribed with 'E. Nesbit Esq'. His collection *English Poems* might have been written for her. Le Gallienne eventually moved to the United States in 1903 but never forgot the words of her poems and would write:

'Her memory has always remained one of my most treasured possessions… All I can do is to recall her as a beautiful inspiring vision and a loved friend.'

If Le Gallienne was extraordinary, Edith's next lover was ordinary. Noel Griffith was a 23-year-old trainee accountant when he met Hubert on a train to Lee. Griffith was reading a book about politics and after they talked about socialism, Hubert invited him to call on the family. Edith was in bed recovering from a miscarriage when he arrived and Griffith was immediately taken with her, later describing her as 'a mixture of sensuality and intellectuality' and 'a very charming and fascinating person'. The next time he visited he brought her some flowers, and Edith was greatly touched by his sweet thoughtfulness. Edith took this straight-laced accountant by the hand and gently introduced him to her bohemian world. A little green around the gills, he was somewhat surprised to walk into her house and straight into a ménage a trois. His diary entry remarked that the family 'rubbed along very friendly' but that Edith found Alice irritating, and Alice was uncomfortable with the domestic arrangement. He described Hubert as, '...very hot blooded... abnormally sexual, too much so for the tastes of his wife.' Liked by both Edith and Hubert, Griffith was invited to join the Blands at their favourite leisure spot on the Medway. This pretty part of the British Isles would become Edith's most beloved holiday destination. Griffith wrote of the time, 'My God! What holidays these were, snatched from a Chartered Accountant's Office. Lots of laughter and lots of good talk.' For four years Edith invited him on holiday, when the party would take a double-scull boat up to East Peckham, near Yalding. Everyone would stay at a pub called the George in the village itself, or The Anchor, which sits on Hampstead Lock, and take a picnic lunch on the river, rowing, walking and swimming in-between. Edith (and Alice) would swim in their clothes, much to Hubert's delight. Edith was an athletic holidaymaker, limboing under a low gate until her head almost touched the ground and diving to the bottom of Yalding Lock to reach a crowbar Hubert had dropped. Other times she strummed her guitar, singing songs that she had composed. In-between, the party would talk politics. Edith wrote about her favourite River Medway and its locks in two romantic novels *Salome and the Head* (1909) and *The Incredible Honeymoon* (1916). All holidays must end sometime and so it was with Edith's fairytale romance with Noel Griffth when he married, started a family and began a new career as a lawyer. He would always stay in touch with Edith, though, and never forgot how she changed his view of the world; he was the only one of her lovers to attend her funeral when she died, later writing:

> 'The old feeling that it was The Blands who had largely moulded my outlook on life never for a moment left me. And of course that inquisitive tolerance has been passed on to my children.
> 'One's outlook was completely changed by such a contact.'

Griffith was friends with three other men – Bower Marsh, Richard Reynolds and Oswald Barron, all clever young men who lived near each other in the Temple in London, all of whom were Fabians and all of whom became Edith's close friends and, possibly, lovers. It seems that Edith didn't always sleep with her conquests; her love for them was perhaps a sort of affectionate fondness rather than a physical passion. She once wrote to her friend H.G. Wells about sex: 'Love is not always the detestable disintegration that you pretend to think it is. Sometimes, & much oftener than you admit it is "nice straight cricket"'. Bower Marsh, like Griffith, was good friends with the Blands and became a regular on their holiday jaunts and Sunday 'at homes'. Edith developed a special tenderness for Marsh, and took him on a date some time in the early 1890s to her beloved childhood home, Halstead Hall. They took a romantic walk through her favourite woods and park surrounding the house, places that were very dear to Edith and that she wanted to share with her young companion. She would compose poetry for him and once painted him a watercolour. Each year for his birthday she posted him her latest volume of poems and in one of the books, Marsh kept two sepia photographs of Edith to remember her by – one rather sexy with her hands behind her head.

In 1893, Edith discovered a new beauty spot at the other end of Kent on the south coast near Hythe, Dymchurch on the Romney Marsh, to which she'd regularly take Bower Marsh and her other lovers. Virtually undiscovered, the fishing village had a pretty windmill and no running water – just a communal pump. At first the Blands stayed at Mill House (as featured in *The New Treasure Seekers*). Later they lodged in a charming little white wooden-and-brick house, which they christened Well Cottage. They invited so many friends to come and stay for the holidays, the family rented another larger house nicknamed The Other House. Nearly opposite, the red-brick property was called Sycamore House; both places were a stone's throw from the beach and it isn't difficult to see the attraction for Edith, a good swimmer. It's easy to imagine how the vast blue of the sea would have cheered and inspired her, as she cycled along the seafront, tea dress billowing behind her. The wide beach was perfect for long walks, smoking and talking with lovers and friends, or playing her favourite game of rounders. At night she would sit on the veranda watching the moonlight on the water and listening happily to the soft sound of the sea on the sand.

Edith and Marsh's affair came to an end when he married in 1901. He introduced her to her next conquest, Richard Reynolds, also an Oxford man, who was head-over-heels in love with her for at least ten years. He would be the last of Edith's young gentlemen for a while and eventually married her niece, Dorothea Deakin. What an incestuous world Edith lived in, making love to four of her husband's friends, who were also friends with Hubert's lover Alice, and eventually pairing one off with her niece!

Edith and Hubert's open marriage seems extraordinary today. Strict morality is what the Victorians are known for but a deeper peep behind society's lace curtain would have revealed debauchery in full swing; prostitution and drunkenness became epidemic in the country during the last half of the nineteenth century as bohemianism gathered momentum. From the outside, Hubert and Edith's relationship is difficult to fathom. Bernard Shaw famously said that no two people were married who were better calculated to make the worst of each other and described Hubert as simultaneously maintaining three wives – Maggie Doran, Edith and Alice Hoatson – all of whom bore him children, with two of the 'wives' living in the same house. Another friend commented that they were better apart but interesting together. Divorce wasn't a choice for Edith (women were considered subservient to men), but even if it had been, it is unlikely she would have taken it. The bohemian beliefs Edith and Hubert shared meant they shunned conventional married life yet remained essentially and fundamentally each other's no matter what happened. Hubert held a great power over Edith and, above everything, they were truly, madly and deeply reliant on each other, both professionally and personally; they were stronger together than apart. Edith was heavily influenced by her husband (as she was by all those she loved), explained her adopted daughter Rosamund after her parents had died. 'His attraction for her and his influence explain so many things that otherwise are not really very comprehensible to anyone who knows human nature for what it is.' Iris believed Alice set herself up as the mistress of the house and contrived Hubert's routine so that Edith hardly had any time with her husband. Rosamund believed Alice and Edith were so close that Hubert thought their friendship was unbreakable.

Edith once described her marriage as a matter of 'two animals mating for animal purposes'. Hubert was vain and simply wouldn't leave women alone and Edith believed that he genuinely couldn't help himself; her general view of men was that their carnal desires must be satisfied somehow. She was quite well-aware of her husband's vanity and if she wanted to get Hubert's attention she would leave a note for him tucked inside the mirror 'where he would be sure to notice it'. Edith once wrote a letter criticising a woman who left her husband because he had a higher sex drive than she did:

> 'That girl you speak of ought not to marry at all, she should be confined in a nunnery or certified under the lunacy act, that sort of woman loose in the world is worse than a pestilence.'

We can only speculate how healthy Edith and Hubert's intimate relationship was. We know that she was a prude (her son revealed this after her death) and that Edith's love affairs with other men were mostly platonic. One of Edith's friends wrote sympathetically about Hubert's unfaithfulness:

'A woman who has maintained husband and home as she did in her early years, has a right to be imperious, but, although myself the most faithful of drudges, I understand to some extent Hubert's flings.'

The friend was Edward Andrade, a physics professor at the University of London who became connected with Edith through his ambitions as a freelance poet. He goes some way to explaining Edith's strange lack of affection, as if she put up a barrier to prevent people from becoming too close to her:

'Looking back, it seems to me both true and remarkable that although many admired her very deeply, found her a wonderful companion and a sympathetic and shrewd friend, a generous hearted woman with a touch of genius, no one ever loved her or felt tender about her as distinct from pitiful and sympathetic. Perhaps tender is not quite the word I want – I mean an emotion which has something of love in it even if not quite love. There was in her that something of the hard and shrewish – so well developed, to the exclusion of nearly everything else…without being unkind.'

The hot-blooded Hubert, for his part, needed sex and confessed he slept with at least fifteen women in the course of his life: to paraphrase him, 'There are many more men who love their wives than there are women who love their husbands,' clarifying this as, 'love them in the true sense of the term, the sense we understand well enough, but cannot minutely define'. Hubert's pursuit of women was not just to sleep with them, but to romance them, enjoy them and make them feel good about themselves before, during and after the affair. 'Make no mistake about it: he was absolutely irresistible to the women he paid court to, not only before the event of capture, but after,' Rosamund, his daughter, would write after her father's death:

'He had a tremendous hold on anyone he had ever possessed. And why? Partly because he took infinite trouble to please and partly because he never looked upon a woman as light 'o love. He was no "he-man", dominating by sheer obvious sexual impulses. He had the sense never to let it look as if it were purely a physical urge on either side. He endowed every affair with the romance of his own imagination. This was a far more deadly lure and a far more efficient trap that the method of the modern cave-man with his snatch and grab stunt, with its intervals of brutal outspokenness and indifference. That doesn't last through a lifetime with any woman, but the other can. Chiefly, through fantasy, perhaps, but what more powerful factor is there in a woman's life, and certainly at that period, than that of fantasy? …'

The irony is that Hubert kept up a strict moral front in public and in his writing, which Bernard Shaw pointed out:

> '[Hubert held] the most severe and rigid sentiments in all sex questions… He would take a violent condemnation tone in denouncing everybody who made any attempt at sexual freedom.'

Hubert always returned to Edith after he slept with other women and was unfailingly polite to her; after all, he believed, 'Fools may make satisfactory lovers, only the wise can make lasting friends.' Edith resigned herself to knowing that she could never be the only woman in his life and took comfort in the fact that Hubert regarded her as the only person in the world who truly understood and loved him. Edith expressed her way of thinking to her good friend, Helen Macklin, who in turn explained:

> 'She invariably assured me that however little he could resist those temptations when they came they were followed by deep repentance and regret; that he could not so hurt her without deep pain afterwards. (That he really loved her in spite of all you know already.) … She wished me to think of him as he was between the lapses. That, she said, was the real man: his heart and his thoughts were sound in spite of his acts, and all I ever saw of him went to confirm her belief.'

Edith found comfort from the deep relationship she enjoyed with Helen, who would come to live with her eventually. Perhaps the affection she felt for and received from friends including Helen helped fill any gap that Hubert left each time he had an affair. Edith's circle of trusted female friends meant a very great deal to her and she always kept up her correspondence with her teenage friend, Ada Breakell; when Ada temporarily moved to Australia, Edith attempted to bridge the geographical distance by encouraging Ada to marry her brother, Harry, who had emigrated to Brisbane. The matchmaking failed but Edith stayed close to Ada and gained significant emotional satisfaction from her, as can be seen from this letter:

'…no one has loved you so long as I – (outside your own people I mean) – and I don't think anyone could love you more. It might be possible to love you better – and yet I don't know that either. I think of you so often of those few minutes in the bedroom at Dulwich. It was then I first felt and realised what it meant for you to be going away. If I live to be a hundred I shall never forget that evening.'

Later in the letter she writes that she even thinks of Ada in her sleep:

'I am always dreaming that I am going to Australia – and I never like it. I hope you like being there – my precious sweetheart. I made the heroine of my last story come from Australia (I was thinking of you).'

She ends her letter to Ada with the heartfelt sign-off, 'Oh my heart – I long for you and love you so – my darling.' In another letter she addresses Ada as 'my soul's own life'. Could Edith have been a lesbian? Probably not. It's true that she attracted both men and women throughout her life but it must be remembered that Edith lived during a time when women expressed their affection for their female friends less self-consciously than we do today. These letters should be read in the context of Victorian emotion rather than through twenty-first century eyes.

The flexibility of Hubert and Edith's marriage worked on some level for the medium-term, allowing Edith to have the time to maintain close friendships with both men and women (platonic or otherwise). She was a busy person with a fulfilling social and professional life; from agreeing to take on every writing job that was thrown at her, to commitments with the Fabian Society, to hosting charity events and parties. Hubert's infidelities caused Edith to seek love from other men and these love affairs kept Edith's belief in romance and magic alive, helping her reassert a sense of control. Further, one particular liaison would have a more significant, and indeed, life-changing function: it revolutionised her writing. Oswald Barron was a civil servant in the public records office and was also a journalist. He would prove to be the most influential of Edith's lovers; as Edith's previous biographer Julia Briggs points out, Barron encouraged Edith to mine the rich memories of her childhood which completely changed her perspective on writing – resulting in extraordinary, overnight, success.

Chapter 9

Finding Treasure

'Real life is often something like books.'

The Story of the Treasure Seekers

Locking the door of her top-floor study, Edith eagerly sat down at the desk. People often described her birdlike, and this morning her eyes looked sprightly and sharp as she inclined her head and picked up her pen. She wasn't alone, and the man whom she had locked in her room was not her husband. Now that Hubert had chosen to concentrate on political journalism, Edith had replaced him with a younger, more creative partner and the relationship was proving successful in more ways than one. Oswald Barron was an erudite young columnist who encouraged her to write like she never had before. He listened for hours as she talked about her childhood adventures across Europe and in rural Kent, and together they wove her tales into a series of brilliant real-life adventure stories with a schoolboy as the narrator. They had an instinct it would sell well.

The Treasure Seekers first appeared in December 1897 in *Father Christmas*, a supplement of the *Illustrated London News* and the adventures of the Bastable children continued in six further instalments over the summer in the *Pall Mall Magazine*. People had read nothing like it before; the misadventures of the six Bastable children from Lewisham was the reality television of its day. Finally, someone was writing about real middle-class children; youngsters who bickered with each other, answered back to grown-ups, had torn clothes, dirty faces and messy hair. These were brothers and sisters who considered that hiding on trains, playing tricks on the neighbours and having dripping for tea was infinitely more fun than doing schoolwork or wearing pretty ringlets and velvet britches. Forget being seen and not heard, these children were shouting loudly and the British reading public was keen to listen. But publishers were yet to be convinced. Edith was sure that the serial would make a successful novel but she was turned down by no less than five editors. She refused to give up and wouldn't negotiate on her terms of a £50 advance with 16.5 per cent royalties. 'Everyone likes the book so much... I am very much in love with it,' she wrote to her agent Morris Colles. Finally, her persistence paid off and in early 1899 Edith was given the news she had been waiting for; she had at last been given a book contract by Fisher Unwin. The company would eventually publish seven more of her novels although she famously distrusted them. *The Story of the Treasure Seekers* was published under the androgynous E. Nesbit just in time for Christmas, illustrated with the original pictures by Gordon Brown from the *Pall Mall Magazine*. It was the best Christmas present Edith could have asked for and made her an overnight success.

After twenty years of hack work, Edith had produced something so extraordinary it established her as the first modern writer for children; *The Story of the Treasure Seekers* changed the way authors wrote for children and even how society viewed the younger generation. Some critics have argued that Edith's direct narrative style has influenced every children's book since. But without Oswald Barron, Edith may never have cracked it. She dedicated the book to him, acknowledging she couldn't have written it without his help. He was her single greatest influence other than her husband, suggests Julia Briggs in her comprehensive analysis of Edith's life, *A Woman of Passion*. Barron was a keen historian and encouraged Edith to make use of her own personal history and especially her unique childhood. It was when Edith concentrated on what had happened to her as a youngster that she tapped into her unique voice and the deep mine of her memory. She began to write authentically about children for children.

Oswald Barron, after whom Oswald Bastable was named, was ten years younger than Edith and he changed her vision of the world. He was, quite literally, the voice of London youth; he wrote a column in the *Evening News* as The Londoner and was witty, lively and wise, too. Edith had met him through her other lovers Bower Marsh and Richard Reynolds; they were friends and neighbours. Barron was also a Fabian and friends with Hubert, who continued to build his success as a political journalist writing increasingly independently from Edith. Barron moved to Grove Park about the same time as the Bland family, and had grown up in Lewisham and Lee. He was treated like one of the family, holidaying at Dymchurch and writing prose and poetry with Edith from around 1892. They wrote a farce, *A Family Novelette*, which was performed in a public hall in New Cross in February 1894. And in the same year they published *The Butler in Bohemia*, a collection of short stories dedicated to their mutual friend Rudyard Kipling. Kipling was another influence on Edith at this time. He had recently published *The Jungle Book* in instalments and the vivid descriptions of talking animals alongside original adventures with a child-centric plot might well have given Edith the inspiration she needed to give her own writing a strong push ahead. *The Jungle Book* is referred to several times in *The Story of the Treasure Seekers*.

Like Kipling, Edith was in the thick of bringing up her own family; by now she had four between 13 and 19 and had first-hand knowledge of exactly what interested children of that time – what games they played, what words they used and what interested them. She based the characters of the Bastables on them mixed in with memories of her two older brothers. Dora is the eldest, followed by Oswald and then Dicky (named after her lover Richard Reynolds), twins Alice and Noel and lastly Horace Octavius (better known as H.O). The story is set in Lewisham, where Edith and Hubert lived when they were first married. When the children's mother dies and the father loses all his money, the family is left in a similar situation as Edith found herself at the beginning of her marriage. But, this time, it is the children who turn the family fortunes around – including hawking magazine stories on Fleet Street by gaslight under the flickering Bovril sign, just as Edith had done as a young mother. Other tales from Edith's childhood appear, such as when the Bastables bury their next-door-neighbour just as Edith was buried as a child in her pretty party dress like a flower by her brothers. There's also the true story of when her own children dressed in their shabbiest clothes to sell flowers they'd picked from the garden to people at the local train station. Even the Bland family's dog, Pincher, makes it into the plot. Perhaps Edith herself appears again as Albert-next-door's uncle, who is a writer and thinks like a child:

> 'He always talks like a book, and yet you can always understand what he means. I think he is more like us, inside of his mind, than most grown-up people are. He can pretend beautifully. I never met anyone else so good at it...'

The children are left alone to run free for most of the book, just as Edith had been allowed to roam the countryside with her brothers; honouring freedom of childhood is something Edith felt strongly about. Another theme close to her heart was of the long-lost parent. Hers had been her father, who died before she was four; the Bastables are without a mother. As Oswald says, '...I saw how different it was from when Mother was here, and we are different, and Father is different, and nothing is like it was.' Later, Oswald comforts his sister Alice, 'She was in that laughey-cryey state when people say things they wouldn't say at other times.' Only someone who has lost a parent could have written those words.

Edith always said she was bored when she was younger, more bored than her mother knew, and she conspires with her readers on this when she writes:

'I am afraid the last chapter was rather dull. It is always dull in books when people talk and talk, and don't do anything, but I was obliged to put it in, or else you wouldn't understand the rest. The best part of books is when things are happening. That is the best part of real things too....'

You can almost hear Edith's voice speaking the words here:

'There are some days when you seem to have got to the end of all the things that could ever possibly happen to you, and you feel you will spend all the rest of your life doing dull things just the same way. Days like this are generally wet days. But, as I said, you never know.'

Edith shows her readers that she remembers even the tiniest moments of being a child, such as pondering over why painting water is always brown and trying to talk when you are about to cry. 'I swallowed that thing that tries to prevent you speaking...' Another time she writes of childhood impatience:

'Dora is rather like grown-ups in that way; she does not seem to understand that when you want a thing you do want it, and that you don't wish to wait, even a minute.'

It is Edith's supreme understanding of human nature, especially a child's nature, that makes the story so brilliant. She sets herself up from the very first line to conspire with her readers by using a boy narrator rather than an adult, adding a humorous twist by not explicitly revealing his identity as Oswald and using the joke as running comedy throughout the novel. Edith treats her readers as equals, using colloquial language with humorous asides and hidden puzzles. She authentically depicts the children's boredom, bickering and being misunderstood and pinpoints exactly what children want to read about – a wild sort of freedom and magical adventures that are real enough to be true.

Ironically, *The Treasure Seekers* was first published under the pen name Ethel Mortimer as Edith already had another story in the same edition of *Pall Mall Magazine*; ironic because the story is so different from anything she had produced so far in her twenty-year career, it may as well have been written by someone else. Writers are always encouraged to develop their unique tone of voice and Edith had finally found hers; she was singing out loud with a distinct, snappy style of diction narrating a very funny story that remains whip-smart more than 100 years after she dreamt it up. The jokes work on different levels; the slapstick for the children and irony for the adults as the children are unknowingly rescued from poverty by a rich friend. The writing seems easy and effortless and, ultimately, the humour is that the Bastables' adventures never turn out like they do in other books. Edith manages a satisfyingly upbeat conclusion without being saccharine (whilst leaving room for an all-important sequel):

> 'The ending is like what happens in Dickens's books… I can't help it if it is like Dickens, because it happens this way. Real life is often something like books.'

Like many bestselling authors, Edith was in the right place at the right time. The idea of writing fiction as entertainment for young readers was just emerging in a culture where families would traditionally read aloud together around the fire after dinner from books of such wide appeal they would be understood by both a toddler and a granny. Literature written for specifically for children began to appear during the last quarter of the nineteenth century when Britain was undergoing tremendous social and political change. As children started to be heard as well as seen, books began to be written about them (and what they got up to behind the closed doors of the nursery) for entertainment rather than education or edification, and distinct from the moralising tales of Christian writers. The golden age of children's literature began in 1860 with Charles Kingsley's *The Water Babies: A Fairy Tale for a Land-Baby* and went on until the Second World War. The canon includes Lewis Carroll's *Alice's Adventures in Wonderland* (1865), Anna Sewell's *Black Beauty* (1877), Beatrix Potter's *Peter Rabbit* (1902), J.M. Barrie's *Peter Pan* (1904), Kenneth Grahame's *The Wind in the Willows* (1908), Frances Hodgson Burnett's *The Secret Garden* (1911) and A.A. Milne's *Winnie-the-Pooh* (1926). American titles include *What Katy Did* (1872) by Susan Coolidge and *The Wizard of Oz* (1900) written by L. Frank Baum. There was a certain amount of crossover with adult fiction – such as Mark Twain's *Tom Sawyer* (1876) and *Adventures of Huckleberry Finn* (1884), Kenneth Grahame's *The Golden Age* (1895) and *Dream Days* (1898), Rudyard Kipling's *Stalky & Co* (1899) and *Little Women* (1868) by Louisa May Alcott. E. Nesbit proudly stands among them all. Hubert wrote about the emergence of children in one of his columns in 1914 called 'The Day of the Child', and perceptively suggested that this change in attitude would be the aspect of the period that would be most remarked upon by later generations. Not mentioning his wife by name, he wrote about the success of books, magazines and plays for young people,

'Some of the largest incomes earned by authors to-day are earned by the authors of children's books.'

Books written specifically for children have an immeasurable importance in a young person's life; it is the first place we read certain vocabulary and can live vicariously through others' adventures. Few of us forget a treasured book from childhood. Yet neither Edith nor her publishers could have predicted the impact *The Story of the Treasure Seekers* would have on generations of readers and authors. She created a blueprint of what children's characters should be – lifelike, adventurous, free from adult constraints – that has been observed by authors from Arthur Ransome to P.J. Travers to Enid Blyton. Edith was the first to use time travel in a children's book; her friend H.G. Wells had published *The Time Machine* in 1895 and she took the concept further when she used the device of a wall as a portal for the Bastables to escape through. This mix of fantasy and reality became a trademark of Edith's unique style, exciting readers of all ages to believe that magic is just around the corner – and might just happen at any moment if we look hard enough. C.S. Lewis, famous for his Chronicles of Narnia of the 1950s, said that Edith Nesbit had a profound influence on his writing. Growing up in Belfast, he devoured her books and was captivated with the idea of children travelling through time and the portal method she used for her characters going into the past and future. In *The Lion, the Witch and the Wardrobe*, he used the bedroom furniture to transport Peter, Susan, Edmund and Lucy, just as Edith used a door in the wall of the park. Perhaps this quote from *The Story of the Treasure Seekers* gave him the idea for his first Narnia novel?

> '...it is so seldom you meet any children who can begin to play right off without having everything explained to them. And even then they will say they are going to 'pretend to be' a lion, or a witch...'

Lewis paid homage to his favourite childhood author when he referenced her in the second paragraph of *The Magician's Nephew* (the seventh book of Narnia), mentioning the Bastable children in the same breath as Arthur Conan Doyle's most famous character, 'In those days Mr Sherlock Holmes was still living in Baker Street and the Bastables were looking for treasure in the Lewisham Road.'

They say life begins at 40 and Edith was in her 40th year when she wrote *The Story of the Treasure Seekers*. The eclectic gifts she received for her birthday show her eccentric personality; who else would receive a pair of pistols along with a fifteenth century gold ring, gloves, a book and some flowers?

Fabian made a bonfire for her and decorated the garden with Chinese lanterns. 'I never feel forty,' Edith wrote to her mother. 'When I am ill I feel ninety – and when I am happy I feel nineteen!'

But what of the person who kickstarted Edith's success? Oswald Barron parted company with her when he married in 1899, the same year *The Treasure Seekers* was published. He would eventually become Britain's leading authority on genealogy and heraldry; his work is still admired in the field today. He was an usher at George V's coronation in 1911 and was given a great honour by being appointed Maltravers herald-extraordinary for the coronation of George VI in 1937. Edith was deeply affected when he married and wrote some of the best poetry of her career around that time, and Barron's influence stayed with her for the rest of her days. She may have been considered middle-aged in Victorian times but her writing was fresh: E. Nesbit had invented an entirely new way of writing children's books, the real-life adventure story, and was about to create another extraordinary literary first.

Chapter 10

Living Well

'An Englishman's house is his castle, of course, but I do wish they built semi-detached villas with moats and drawbridges.'

The Railway Children

In a rural hamlet of south-east London, a country lane wound past fields strewn with wild flowers, hawthorn and chestnut trees. Half mile or so from the village church, tucked away behind a thick holly hedge, an eighteenth century gentleman's residence stood at the corner of the long road to Woolwich Common and the lane to Kidbrooke. Well Hall was magnificent; three storeys high and set in seven and a half acres of orchards and glorious gardens. It was covered in ivy and surrounded by a Tudor moat and bridge that had been there even before Hampton Court. Situated in the village of Eltham, with its population of a few hundred farming folk, the mansion was flanked by woods on one side, open farmland on the other and overlooked by a castle on Shooter's Hill. It was just the sort of grand, wild and romantic place that a children's author might dream about – and Edith fell in love with Well Hall as soon as she saw it. It would be the home she would live in the longest (for 23 years, from 1899 to 1922) and the place in which she wrote her most famous books including *The Railway Children* and *Five Children and It.*

The apple tree blossom was just coming into bud that day in May when the Bland family moved house and Edith was blooming too; she was 41 and pregnant again. Paul was 19, Iris was 17, Fabian was 14 and Rosamund, just entering her teenage years at 13; they yelled with delight when they saw their new home for the first time. Jumping down from the cart, they ran along the driveway that curled around the circular lawn into the overgrown jungle of the garden. Shrieking, they raced by the old red-brick walls, playing hide and seek amongst the beds that were bursting with cottage flowers of iris, wild briar, honeysuckle, columbine and berberis. Gnarled apple trees grew alongside birch and oak trees while white mulberry nestled next to whitebeam and alder trees.

Edith and Hubert followed their children, walking arm in arm under the two ancient cedar trees whose boughs almost touched their bedroom window. They had been told that the saplings had been planted from Lebanon three hundred years before; how inviting they looked to sit under and write. Edith's heart had always been in the countryside; after all, her poetry was inspired by rural England, she loved holidaying in the wilds of Kent and her young teenage years at Halstead Hall had been her happiest. Her moods had always been affected by the seasons, 'The spring always makes me quite drunk with love of her,' she once wrote to her agent. She wanted to recreate her joyful childhood and this house was deep in the countryside yet not too far from the city where she and Hubert commuted regularly for work. The money Edith had made from *The Story of the Treasure Seekers* allowed her to move everyone out of the capital; finally, they escaped to the country after years of suburban London with its grime and narrow-mindedness. Although they didn't own Well Hall (the Blands continued to rent), it was Edith's dream home and forever house, and one that gave her the space, freedom and inspiration to express herself both in her writing and her lifestyle.

The family walked together towards the mansion, across the lawn and over the medieval bridge that crossed the moat overhung with weeping willow. How much they would all come to love that moat. It would be the place Edith wrote her best work, sitting for hours in the punt, thinking, dreaming and scribbling as she gently bobbed in the water. The children would spend all summer swimming in its waters and making rafts, and ice-skating on it in winter. As the Blands walked through the front door of their new home for the first time, they came into the grand hall with its black and white chequered marble floor and large panelled glass window. A huge oak staircase stood in the centre, and bedrooms came off on either side as the main house had been extended with wings. It was very crumbly by the time the Blands arrived; the wrought-iron balcony at the back of the house was falling down and the staircase was so wobbly it collapsed soon after they moved in. There was no proper plumbing, the roof leaked and the place was so damp and rotting that coal fires were immediately burned for hours to get rid of the smell of decay. Cooking was basic to say the least, and put off many of the staff that came to work there. But Edith and Hubert couldn't have been happier with it and took it all to be part of the charm of the eccentric old place, setting to work to make it a comfortable family home. Edith adored interior decorating and antiques and it didn't take her long to furnish the thirty rooms in the comfortable, faded-luxury of the early Victorian style. The hall was decorated with dark oak and old brass; on the first floor was a small library that she stocked with her own books as well as family favourites of Dickens, Thackeray, Hardy,

Fielding, Eliot, Brontë and Austen. Edith loved chandeliers and we can guess from her fictional writing that she furnished her enormous upstairs drawing room with its view of the gardens with colourful (perhaps purple) sofas, blue tapestries, vivid scarlet wall hangings, yellow-gold ornaments and faded needlework cushions. The fireplace was shielded with a screen of old-world design and elsewhere stood a table of papier-mâché and mother of pearl, surrounded by straight-backed chairs with twisted feet. An oak bureau with brass handles overflowed with Edith and Hubert's manuscripts, although the couple worked separately in different rooms. Hubert's study was at the front of the house facing the new railway line and Edith's desk faced the garden at the back of the property, overlooking the glorious old rose bushes. It is said that Edith stamped her individuality on every room that she ever lived in and she especially enjoyed scouring second-hand shops and Caledonian Market in north London for china; she had good taste with a keen eye for a bargain. She collected bohemian glass lustres (table decorations with hanging prisms) and other knick-knacks including rare pink china, green Venice glasses and silver goblets. The finishing touch was added over the mantelpiece in Hubert and Edith's bedroom; a poem by Swinburne, written in curling calligraphy, framed in ivy leaves and decorated with a skull, that summed up their bohemian life together:

> 'From too much love of living,
> From hope and fear set free,
> We thank with brief thanksgiving
> Whatever gods may be
>
> That no man lives for ever;
> That dead men rise up never;
> That even the weariest river
> Winds somewhere safe to sea.'

More space meant more animals. Edith had always been a dog-lover and now she had a huge garden for her pets to run about in. She had a large number of dogs throughout her life and dachshunds were her favourite to spoil. She would usually have several around the table at mealtimes and would lift two on her lap; when she got down after eating, she would often forget about the numerous leads tied to her chair and trip over. Over dinner she would no doubt have entertained many a guest with the remarkable real tale of her dog, Baby, who travelled on the train from London to Manchester when Edith made a visit to her sister and mother. Baby was chained up in the carriage for pets but managed to escape when the train stopped at Derby. He eventually found his way back to London five days later, thin, ragged and dirty. Edith used her beloved dachshunds Max and Brenda as characters in *The Magic City* (1910) – although famously they were misdrawn as Dalmatians. Edith's beloved Well Hall became a character in many of her novels including *The Would-Be-Goods* (1901), *The Red House* (1902) and *The Lark* (1922). *Salome and the Head* (1909), was inspired by the house's history; in the sixteenth century it had been the home of Sir Thomas More's daughter, Margaret (apparently More's severed head was buried in the garden) and, later, the watchmaker John Arnold, who researched the concept of Greenwich longitude. The house had also been a school; even today the old bell can still be seen hanging from the Tudor barn.

Entertaining guests was Edith's favourite thing to do, and she and Hubert adored sharing their rural idyll with their friends from a circle that grew wider and more varied. For his part, Hubert enjoyed playing up to the role of country gentleman and became a keen gardener, especially of roses. Their door was always open and Edith loved it when friends dropped in unannounced to ask for her help and advice, or to use Well Hall as a retreat to finish some writing project or other. On a sunny morning a fellow or two might take the train down from London for a game of badminton or to play tennis on the lawn, or to take the punt out on the moat. The story goes that a band of Edith's young gentlemen friends tipped up one afternoon to build a raft for her from old bits of fencing they put together and tarred. Placing a wicker chair proudly on their vessel, they invited Edith to go on a maiden voyage. Dressed in her best Liberty dress, she grandly stepped aboard – only for it to capsize straight away and ruin the frock. Apparently, Edith was the most amused of them all. For four years Edith and Hubert's large and frequent weekend house parties became legendary, 'the party never flagged once the Blands had appeared. A friendly atmosphere hung about them, an atmosphere of festivity. They were intensely lovable,' wrote one guest. The company was wildly eclectic, described by another friend as gatherings of 'enthusiastic youth, flaming socialists and decorous Fabians'. Essayists, novelists, leader writers, critics and journalists all rubbed shoulders together. H.G. Wells once remarked that Well Hall was 'a place to which one rushed down from town at the week-end to snatch one's bed before anyone else got it'. Guests would catch the train from Cannon Street via Blackheath on a Friday and beds would be claimed first-come, first-served. If people arrived early, Edith might still be working on a chapter and Hubert would be finishing his column for the *Chronicle,* so friends were expected to let themselves in the rear servants' entrance from the moat garden – they were discouraged from coming in through the front door where the long dining table was laid out by a sign announcing 'The Front Door is at the Back'. Once inside, guests would be welcomed into their rooms with verses written for them by Edith, and small posies of flowers she had made up. Before dinner, guests were set to work to collect Hubert's roses from the garden in wicker washing baskets; the flowers were made into a sort of mat to decorate the long dining table and twisted around the silver candlestick centrepieces. Imagine the fragrance! Edith wrote about this in *The Railway Children*, when Roberta's birthday tea plates were decorated in the same sort of way. Flowers were important to Edith because they helped her abide by her personal mantra which was 'to live beautifully' – she would tie knots of jasmine behind her children's ears, and encouraged them to offer leftover roses to people passing by Well Hall the next day.

Once everything was perfect for the party, Edith would finally appear, radiant, on the grand staircase. To the embarrassment of some guests and the delight of others she would sweep down to greet them wearing Turkish slippers and her trademark Liberty silk gown – loose, long and flowery; sometimes in faded old-fashioned colours, other times in peacock blue. Strings of amber beads dripped from her neck and silver bangles jangled on her arm as she smoked from her long cigarette holder. Her dark shiny hair was parted smoothly and her face would be a picture of pure joy to see all her 'darlings' gathered to see her. Edith had always had something of the theatrical about her and as she grew older, more successful and more confident, she played up to the part of the glamorous hostess. As everyone sat down to dinner, adoring young men, dazzled by her vitality and magnificent appearance, would surround Edith. The meal would be late and leisurely, and, depending on finances, simple or extravagant. One particularly fine supper was served by two Swiss chefs who made each guest a pudding of small sugar chalets lit from inside with a candle. More regularly it was good plain food, such as bean soup followed by cheese and apples from the garden. No matter the fare, wine always flowed freely, served from her favourite Venetian glass bottles. Edith was always thrilled to see her wide and varied circle of young (and old) things mixing freely and sharing good conversation. Everyone, including her children, had their turn to express their views. Hubert enjoyed this part of the evening the most. While he didn't care for dancing and was mildly embarrassed about his wife's amateur dramatics, he spoke as he wrote; he was a vain person who loved the sound of his own voice but was also a good listener who enjoyed hearing the ideas of the young guests. Often amongst the party would be a person taking shelter at Well Hall, such as a fledgling artist or writer or a poor relation. 'No one who knew the Blands could resist seeking their comfort and their counsels in distress,' wrote one friend. 'Not only in giving help to others, but in heart and generous judgement, she was lavishly kind, and full of allowance for the failing and misdoings of those for whom she felt affection, she was warm and enthusiastic to a fault...' wrote another.

After dinner, the carpet would be rolled back for games such as charades, forfeits or a scary version of hide-and-seek for adults that Edith invented called devil in the dark, which eventually had to be banned because players destroyed so much furniture. Edith wasn't shy about after-dinner speaking and was known as a good mimic and speaker albeit with a cutting and sarcastic manner. During one infamous game of forfeits played with H.G. Wells, the dramatist and writer Laurence Housman was blindfolded and had to find a lady's shoe. Wells quipped, 'It's no use looking for my wife's feet – she hasn't any; she goes on castors.' Edith loved talking late into the night, usually drowsing in her chair while the conversation went on around her. But if she was displeased with what she heard, watch out – she would give a low hiss. Singing and dancing were another post-dinner favourite as Edith, cigarette dangling from her lips, would sit on a piano stool with her Liberty draperies streaming over it, playing old-world favourites such as *Greensleeves* and *Auld Lang Syne*, while daughter Rosamund sang. Edith loved showing off in front of her friends, performing plays she had written in her rich, theatrical voice. Edith could have been an actress – after all, she played plenty of roles in her life; writer, mother, patron, wife and lover – and had written under all sorts of pen-names before becoming established as E. Nesbit: Daisy Nesbit, Edith Nesbit, Edith Band, and Fabian Bland (with Hubert). Now in her forties, Edith's friends never called her by her first name but nicknamed her Duchess, Dear Duchess and Madame. (Hubert's pet name for her had always been Cat.) As she became a successful author, Edith took on the mantle of actress – in public she was a wholesome champion of children; in private she was an eccentric bohemian who believed that 'Drama, drama keeps women going'. H.G. Wells commented in *Experiment in Autobiography*, Victor Gollancz Ltd (1932) that Edith was self-aware enough to recognise her penchant for fantasy:

> 'E. Nesbit, bye the bye, did some short stories in which she dealt with this same unreality in the world as she knew it. She saw through herself enough for that. They are collected together under the title of *The Literary Sense*.'

LIVING WELL

Laurence Housman wrote:

> 'Indeed she had so much of a 'presence', that a certain amount
> of "pose" came naturally to her, and that without any insincerity.'

As Britain moved from the nineteenth into the twentieth century, Well Hall became a colourful country bohemian bolthole and Edith was crowned the period's original party girl. No one could describe her without using the words 'very kind' or 'very generous' and she and Hubert became famous for their hospitality – a generosity that would lead them into financial ruin. Usually the late-night antics meant guests would miss their last trains and had to sleep where they could, with the men bunking down in the garden cottages. The unspoken rule was that everyone should leave early without seeing Edith or Hubert, perhaps catching breakfast with their son Paul (who was now out to work as a stockbroker in the city), before vanishing until the next party. Iris would go off to the Slade School of Fine Art, and the teenagers Fabian and Rosamund were away at school. Edith would eventually emerge after everyone had gone, the house quiet after all the laughing, dancing and joy. Reluctantly, she would get back to her writing, forcing herself to get through as many as five thousand words a day, depending how late she was with her deadline. Later she might be seen out of doors, doing some hefty gardening or playing a hard game of badminton. The fantasy of the previous night's party was over and Edith didn't welcome the cold light of day, for behind all the warm friendships, dinner parties and joyful games, hid a family under strain. While Edith had miscarried, Alice was pregnant again and there are no prizes for guessing who the father was. Hubert and Alice's second illegitimate child was born the same year they moved to Well Hall on 6 October 1899 – in secret again, twelve miles away at a private address of 21, Woolwich Road in Bexleyheath. They named their son John Richard Rhodes on his birth certificate, born to John and Marcia Hoatson, (formerly Bland) although his middle and surnames were later changed to Oliver Wentworth Bland. When she saw the helpless new-born, Edith once again found it in her heart to adopt him as one of her own, allowing Alice to love him behind closed doors. Accepting the illegitimate Rosamund 13 years before had been Edith's act of loyalty to Hubert and an extraordinary gesture of generosity to Alice; when Edith was betrayed for a second time, her compassion was truly heroic and showed that the love she felt for her husband was so great it could overcome any obstacle. For her, life without him was unthinkable and she would rather share him with Alice that not have him at all. As Hubert himself once wrote in his column, 'It is better for women to be married than not. Better have a bad husband than none, eh?' Hubert felt contrition for his acts of unfaithfulness with Alice, and it would have taken all his powers of patience to calm down Edith's overwhelming distress. They may have had an open marriage but Edith was easily hurt and would cry often; years of smoking cigarettes didn't help her nerves and she started to develop a horrendous temper. Hubert was the only person who could control her, knowing exactly the sort of soothing phrases that would coax his wife from sobbing behind slammed doors. Edith was aware of her fault and always felt deep remorse after her 'blights' as she called them, emerging from anger with apologies and kisses for all she had hurt. Alice Hoatson, the Mouse, standing silently in the background, quietly witnessed all the tears and heart-wringings and suffered tortures over what she had done.

Hubert loved his wife more than everyone else but not instead of everyone else. He was a true romantic in the sense that he adored all women, not just Edith. He vainly saw himself as one of the noble knights that William Morris wrote about, and women were his fair damsels; the garden at Well Hall was his Eden and the females who walked through it were a constant temptation. 'I confess I have always greatly preferred women to men. They are nicer to look at and to talk to,' he wrote in his *Hubert* column. He argued that marriage was important for producing families but it took the fine edge off life. He wrote:

'I have never proposed to abolish it [marriage]… only to alter it a trifle. Romance, in-loveness, cannot survive six weeks of the appalling intimacy of marriage… The thing that should follow is friendship… friendship touched by intimacy…

Hubert suggesting married people should see less of each other and perhaps live in different places (as he did early on in his marriage). He believed women get more out of being married than men do and that life is a continual compromise 'in which there must be ever so much more give than take'. He believed that a man's infidelity was punished out of all proportion and wrote about such moral dilemmas:

'Are there not in each of us two selves? The little Self and the big Self; the low Self and the high Self; the Self that is always for dabbling in the mud and the Self that arches towards the stars?'

Perhaps reflecting on his own marriage, he warned against tying the knot for passion, as he and Edith had done:

> '…to marry in haste is to do something more than to prepare for oneself a leisured repentance: it is in all probability to bring into the world offspring whose lives will be one long expiation of their parents' ghastly error.'

Edith's turmoil over this strange domestic love triangle caused her the sort of emotional pain that would surface as resentment so great that it eventually threatened her entire relationship with her children. Having lost her father as an infant, Edith had always yearned for the stability of unconditional love and this became a common theme in her writing. These stories for children have a happy ending but Edith also wrote about what happens when lost love can never be recovered. The result was altogether different. E. Nesbit's horror and ghost short stories have largely been forgotten by modern readers yet are amongst the most readable, powerful and memorable of her adult fiction. She is known for being the first modern author for children but she should also be applauded for her pioneering ghost stories that were several degrees chillier than anything that had been written before.

Edith mostly wrote her tales of terror in the late 1880s and they are outstanding for their concise turn of phrase, genuinely horrible plotlines and gruesome conclusions that linger with the reader long after bedtime. They also reveal the mind of someone who wasn't in a happy place. Many of the stories centre around the deep sadness of unrequited love between a man and a woman, a sadness that manifests itself in psychologically disturbing ways when love letters are written in blood and a dismembered plait is all that remains of an affair. Throats are cut, vampires prey, lovers return from the dead and Dr Frankenstein-style experiments are performed. The motifs Edith uses are now regarded as classic components of ghost stories – corpses lying under white sheets, skulls and skeletons. Edith was fascinated with the supernatural throughout her life; highly superstitious, she believed in black magic and at least two of her houses were said to be haunted including Well Hall with one room in particular that frightened her children. She always kept a skull on the mantelpiece to try to normalise death and all that was associated with it, although it didn't seem to work as she would often scare herself silly writing late at night and wake up the household to sit with her or play badminton in the garden until it got light. Although she was determined to overcome her childhood fear of the dark when her own family was born, Edith's anxiety regularly pops up along with her preoccupation of being buried alive, apparently stemming from her grandfather who had been in his coffin and was about to be put in the ground when he was found to be still breathing. Edith's imagination for horror was so vivid she recalled several incidents from her childhood and wove them into her fiction, including her obsession with the waxworks of Madame Tussauds and the mummies of Bordeaux she encountered in France. As she wrote of one of her characters, 'in his brain the fear of death beating like a hammer'; so it was for Edith.

One of her most famous and well-written stories is 'Man-Size in Marble' (1893, in the collection *Grim Tales*, A.D. Innes & Co.) in which a pair of newlyweds blissfully set up home in the countryside before being savagely torn apart by an ancient local superstition. Edith came up with the idea after one of her holidays on the Romney Marshes when she came across Brenzett Church and saw two life-size marble statues as a monument to the civil war. The story is all the more chilling for its authenticity; the sharpness of the narrative leaves the reader with a real taste of horror in their mouth as the unforgettable punch line is delivered. Elsewhere, albeit perhaps subconsciously, Edith worked through her emotional trauma by re-writing and re-imagining her own dramatic love life. Is it Alice Hoatson who is referred to in 'The Shadow', as the silent omnipresent housekeeper Miss Eastwich who is 'model of decorum and decently done duties' whose 'pale eyes went through my heart like a knife'? When Miss Eastwich is invited by her two only friends to their newlywed home, she is left alone with the husband as the wife goes up early to bed. As the pair sit together in the dining room each side of the fireplace, the husband tells her the house is haunted. 'You were always so sensible and strong-minded, and Mabel's like a little bird on a flower.' Miss Eastwich says of the husband, 'His was not a very strong character; very sweet and kind, and gentle, but not strong. He was always easily led.' The end leaves the reader with a sorrowful image of Miss Eastwich and her illegitimate daughter in a grotesque transmutation of Edith, Hubert and Alice's ménage a trois. In another mood, it is possible that Edith's wild imagination elevated her love for Hubert to a *Wuthering Heights*-type tragedy in the powerful 'Hurst of Heathcote'. When a lover must die to release the soul of his lost betrothed, Edith writes herself as a sort of hysterical Cathy and Hubert as Heathcliff (perhaps silently pencilling in Alice as the insipid Linton character). Shades of Charlotte Brontë also appear in the description of the landscape in another story, 'The Violet Car', as Edith writes of the wilderness of Kent in much the same way as Brontë wrote about rural Yorkshire. Well Hall is regularly part of Edith's landscape of horror, with plots that suggest she felt alone, isolated and terrified in the huge Tudor mansion. From burglars to ghostly trespassers, she seems obsessed with fear of the unknown as Well Hall's most charming aspects seen in the sunshine are transmuted into gothic horrors at night as ghosts rise from the moat, the ivy that covers the wall becomes a deadly man-strangling vine and owls hoot ominously from the cedar trees.

Edith mostly wrote her ghost stories as pot-boilers for magazines, yet they are far more readable than much of her other adult fiction and reveal the tremendous intellect of someone who could create genuinely gruesome tales alongside the happiest, most carefree children's stories. Edith had a split personality and these stories are an expression of how she really felt about her complicated domestic situation. The most dreadful part about Edith's preoccupation with long-lost love is that her fear was about to become horrifically real in a twist of fate far more awful than anything she could have imagined. 'They talk about death being cold. It's life that's the cold thing…' she wrote in 'The Detective': little did she know what was around the corner.

Chapter 11

Death of a Son

The Devil's Due
'And every flower dropped its head
And all the rose's leaves were shed,
And all the lilies dropped down dead.'
    Lays and Legends by E.Nesbit, Longmans, Green & Co (1886)

Edith was going out of her mind. Day and night she was haunted by his face, the whisper of his voice. She took long walks in the country and his figure was always just round the next turn of the road, in the next glade of the wood. But she never found him, the beloved, lost son who would never come back to her. Just as her father had never returned.

Fabian at 15 years old was an exceptionally brilliant boy and the child whom Edith thought was most like her in character, although he resembled his father in looks. Educated at Scotland's oldest boarding school, Loretto, he was wayward and daring, getting into constant trouble with his father. Described as 'amazing' and 'a terror', his nickname at school was Bloodthirsty Bill. Three months before his sixteenth birthday, Fabian was due to have an operation to remove his adenoids because he had been suffering a string of heavy colds. It was considered a routine operation and the family had arranged with their doctor for it to be done at home. The event seemed so insignificant to the Blands that everyone forgot about it until the doctor and anaesthetist arrived at 11am on Thursday 18 October 1900. Fabian was digging in the garden in his oldest clothes and Edith was still in bed. They both hurried to get washed and dressed before the operation began in Fabian's bedroom.

Before lunchtime the medics were satisfied the operation had gone well and left Fabian to wake up from the anaesthetic in his bedroom. But the boy was never to breathe again; his young teenage body, once full of life, was now extinguished forever. It was Hubert who discovered him at about 1pm, body cold and arms and legs already stiff. 'They've killed him,' he cried out to Alice, running into the library and reaching for the drinks decanter. Alice, who was cleaning, ran in horror to Fabian's bedroom but couldn't wake him. The house was in a state of confusion; no one could understand what had happened. When Edith heard the unthinkable news, she rushed to her son and desperately tried to warm up his lifeless body with hot water bottles and 16 candles. At first, she couldn't bring herself to believe the worst and kept repeating to Alice, 'I wish you'd told me what would happen.' But as the muscles on Fabian's face set, Edith had no choice but to call for an undertaker. Coming downstairs, she saw the table set with Fabian's place and, knowing her son would never again sit with the family, she became hysterical. She screamed at Hubert in the midst of her agony and grief, 'Why couldn't it have been Rosamund?' The poor girl heard her mother and at that moment began to guess there was some sort of secret surrounding her birth. She had always felt Edith had treated her differently from the others and now her adopted mother's resentment started to make sense:

> 'I was aware of it all through my childhood and as I didn't know the cause until I was eighteen [five years after Fabian's death] it was always a source of bewilderment to me... It wasn't just that she did not feel for me what she felt for her own children. How could she? She actually, I think, always subconsciously, at any rate, had a lot against me. She did not forgive my existence. To John she was quite different. Somehow she never felt he was in competition with her own children as I had been and it may have been partly that that made the difference.'

For years, Edith was ignorant that her adopted daughter suspected the truth of her birth but Rosamund never forgave her. One further person was drawn into the Bland's greatest secret when Fabian died. Helen Macklin, one of Edith's most trusted friends, was staying at Well Hall that fateful day. In the throes of bitterness, Edith told her everything, as Helen later wrote:

> '...she told me the bare facts in a burst of grief on the night of Fabian's death. But the next day she said more and often afterwards – since I now knew – she gave herself the relief of speaking to me about it.'

The concealment that Edith, Hubert and Alice had carefully maintained for eighteen years had been finally let out, yet Macklin breathed not a word to anyone and the farcical ménage a trois continued for a further thirteen years.

Rosamund may have been in turmoil over the truth of her birth but later that month she put it behind her to join the family huddled together as they tearfully made the cold, weary journey up the hill to the local parish church to lay their beloved Fabian to rest in the graveyard of St John the Baptist in Eltham. It's a mystery why no headstone marks his body – perhaps Edith and Hubert had laid a wooden cross for him that has long since perished. Fabian's death certificate records the post-mortem verdict: 'Syncope [loss of consciousness] following administration of chloroform properly administered for performance of necessary operation.' It is thought that the poor boy died by choking on vomit as he began to regain consciousness. Everyone had forgotten that he shouldn't consume food or drink in the 24 hours before his operation and he probably had eaten breakfast that morning and dinner the night before. Edith, now 42, never forgave herself for Fabian's death and descended into near madness over it. She was haunted by his face and voice as her mind began to play tricks on her, the deep sadness of her father's sudden death resurfacing. At three years old, Edith had lost a beloved male figure in her life and now her son had died. It was an unbearable Christmas. 'I don't know how I got through those long weeks and months. I tried to write; I tried to read; I tried to live the life of a reasonable human being. But it was impossible,' Edith wrote in one of her ghost stories. 'I tell you there are some things that cannot be written about. My life for those long months was one of them…' A sort of dullness dimmed Edith's bright hazel eyes as she lost interest in everything. She stopped going to Fabian Society meetings and no letters to her friends, mother or brother survive from this time. When the day of what would have been Fabian's sixteenth birthday arrived on 8 January, her guilt was so great it would gnaw at her soul for the rest of her life. 'It is not the dead who are to be pitied most,' she once wrote. As the cold winter drew on, the moat at Well Hall froze over like hell and Hubert was suffering too. He possibly contemplated suicide, 'Life… so far from being a state of enjoyment, is always, and necessarily, one of suffering… Life is a struggle for existence with the certainty of being vanquished,' he once wrote in his *Hubert* column. To help him cope, Hubert turned to the church and found comfort in Catholicism. He converted and put his trust in God:

> 'We do well to realise that we live in a real and not an ideal world;
> a world that was already made for us when we came into it, a
> world that we have done nothing whatever to make and that we
> can do precious little to alter. This world, this rummy jumble of

Well Hall in Eltham, Edith and Hubert's celebrated Edwardian party palace, complete with moat and resident ghost; they lived here for 23 years from 1899.

Rosamund with the family's dogs. Edith adored canines.

Clockwise from top left: Edith's children; Fabian, Iris, Paul and Rosamund (baby John on next page).

Above left: Alice Hoatson, holding John.

Above right: Edith and Hubert's wide circle of friends included literary great George Bernard Shaw.

Below left: Edith in the drawing room of Well Hall, taken for *Tatler* magazine in 1904.

Below right: Edith writing at her desk at the peak of her powers, aged 45.

The Psammead from *Five Children and It* (1902), brought to life by illustrator HR Millar.

Hubert Bland, one of the most well-known journalists of his time and Edith's husband for better or worse.

In 1912 Edith met her public at
Olympia when she was part of an
exhibition.

Edith adored her only
grandchild, Pandora, born
in 1908.

Above left: Edith's final romantic hero and second husband, Tommy Tucker, pictured with a pet parrot.

Above right: St Peter the Apostle Roman Catholic Church in Woolwich where Edith and Tommy married in February 1917.

Below: Edith's last home The Long Boat and The Jolly Boat, where she died in 1924.

Edith is buried at St Mary's-in-the-Marsh in Kent with a traditional naval wooden memorial made by Tommy.

A new generation fell in love with the Psammead after the BBC's 1991 television series.

Jenny Agutter as Bobbie, Sally Thomsett as Phyllis and Gary Warren as Peter starred in the phenomenally popular 1970 film *The Railway Children*. Agutter played the character of Mother in the 2000 film.

Left: Dame Jacqueline Wilson brought renewed attention to Edith Nesbit when she wrote *Four Children and It* in 2012. She is pictured at Well Hall unveiling the wooden sculpture of the Psammead, commissioned by the Edith Nesbit Society in 2013.

Below: A contemporary painting of *The Railway Children* by Skye Davis of Prendergast Vale School in Lewisham, near Edith's former home in Elswick Road.

a world, we must take more or less for granted. We can leave it, of course, but if we decide to stay in it we must stay in it on its terms and not on ours. It is not, as Mr H.G. Wells suggests it is, a lump of clay which we can take into our hands, and mould to our pattern. On the contrary, it is we who are the clay, and it is the world who will do most of the moulding. The best we can hope for is to get just a little bit of our own way.'

As Hubert found the strength to deal with the loss of Fabian, Edith dug deep within and forced herself to work again. What a tremendous effort it must have taken to screw up every ounce of her courage and put pen to paper, turning a mind heavy with grief to light-hearted stories of jolly children and their cheerful adventures. Writing systematically had never come easy to her, she usually worked in fit and starts, but she had a deadline for the *Illustrated London News* of ten stories about the further adventures of Oswald Bastable and family and so she had no choice but to hunker down and throw herself into work. She managed to finish the first episode in little over a month after Fabian's death. Writing proved to be Edith's salvation, a coping mechanism for the awfulness of her loss, as she forced herself to dream up other worlds where she could wipe the slate of life clean and re-write it as a happy place with healthy children. Day after day she sat at her desk, writing in her distinct, feminine, looping handwriting on squares of green paper, throwing down sheet after sheet as she filled them up and creating a sea of stories all around her chair. As the daylight dimmed and her thoughts were at risk of turning dark, she would gather up the thin papers, put them in order (she always wrote the page number in the top right-hand corner) and pinned them together with a paper clip. After a few days she would re-read her work, make just a few amendments, and submit the story to her editor. So confident was Edith in her writing that she didn't waste time agonising over plot lines or characters; her quick intelligence, good judgement and instinct meant she wrote efficiently. Perhaps it was her deep sadness too, that focused her mind to get the job done; with the loss of Fabian, life had been brought into sharp focus and suddenly become more precious.

It would be those very words she wrote in deep grief that would become her most successful. The second collection of adventures about the Bastables were eventually published as *The Would-Be-Goods,* almost exactly a year after her son's death, in Christmas 1901 and dedicated to him. The novel turned out to be the greatest financial success of her career and she earnt £1,100 pounds in royalties alone in just a year – about £57,000 in today's money. Edith drew on the familiar for *The Would-Be-Goods,* setting the story around the Moat House (Well Hall in disguise) with the five children resolving to set up a club to be good. The capers never turn out as intended, of course, with dancing goats, lost Roman antiquities and a misplaced baby. The adventures are Edith's funniest so far; she clearly found humour a way to get through those dark days of pain. Grief lurks in the background theme as the children's mother has died; at one point, Oswald remembers how his mother loved flowers and wished she could see their garden, 'But it is no use wishing.' Death is discussed elsewhere in the episode when the Bastables try to comfort a widow whose son has been killed in the Boer War:

> 'We wanted to do something for the soldier's mother, but you can do nothing when people's sons are shot. It is the most dreadful thing to want to do something for people who are unhappy, and not to know what to do.'

Yet more unhappiness would befall Edith almost exactly two years after she laid Fabian to rest. In mid-December 1902, her mother Sarah passed away of old age, at the home of her son-in-law John Deakin, Booths Hall in Worsley, Lancashire. She was 84. It must have been a relief in some ways for Mrs Nesbit, who had known the heartbreak of four of her six children dying before she did, Saretta, her eldest daughter, having died suddenly on 25 October 1899. Edith was deeply upset as she adored her mother and they had always enjoyed a close relationship, despite their vast personality differences and Sarah's dislike of Hubert. Sarah had lived with her daughter when Edith was a struggling young mother in Lewisham and Lee, and Edith always thought of her gentle and kind mother fondly, lovingly nicknaming her 'the old mother owl'. Sarah was proud of her daughter's success; although she would never know quite how famous she became. Edith always made a point of sending her the first copy of each of her published books, signing off as 'Daisy', her mother's pet name for her. The tender recollection of the special relationship between mother and child is something Edith often wrote about, and her mother would most especially inspire her to write *These Little Ones* in 1909. Edith once wrote:

> 'Since my Mother died things come back to me from years ago – little things that I might have done for her and did not do. And I would give the world if I had done those little things.'

In the years that followed the death of Fabian and her mother, Edith's grief mixed with remorse provided her with a tremendous impetus with which to write. Over seven years she produced her best work and wrote an impressive nine novels and one collection of short stories – four written in the same year – including *The Red House* (1902), *The Phoenix and the Carpet* (1904), *The New Treasure Seekers* (1904), *The Story of the Amulet* (1906), *The Railway Children* (1906), *The Incomplete Amorist* (1906) and *The Enchanted Castle* (1907). It was the book that Edith wrote in 1902 that would produce her most memorable character; a creature which, despite its worldwide fame, doesn't even possess a proper name.

Chapter 12

It

'She could be as cantankerous as her own cantankerous Psammead...' - A friend's description of Edith.

Five Children and It was originally published as *The Psammead* as a series of nine episodes in the *Strand Magazine* running from April to December 1902 and inspired two sequels, *The Phoenix and the Carpet* (1904) and *The Story of the Amulet* (1906). Mixing fantasy into a story about real children had never been done before and this idea has influenced almost every successful children's author since, from C.S. Lewis to J.K. Rowling. A generation before Edith, the phantasmagorical imagination of a maths lecturer at Oxford University had dreamed up the surreal tales of *Alice's Adventures in Wonderland* (1865). Charles Lutwidge Dodgson, better known by his pen name of Lewis Carroll, experimented with fantasy and reality but it could be argued that Edith Nesbit pioneered the idea because she grounded her escapist adventures – and their consequences – in middle-class reality. Cyril, Anthea, Robert, Jane and their baby brother are depicted so vividly they remind the reader of themselves; they argue with each other and wish for the things we'd all wish for, such as to be beautiful, become rich or to fly. The children's reactions to the nasty consequences of these wishes are equally believable.

Edith based the characters of *Five Children and It* on her own five children, fictionally written as first cousins once removed from the Bastables. The Lamb was Edith's youngest, John, who shared that nickname and was always held in great affection by the family. Her eldest child, Paul had a middle name of Cyril, the name of the eldest brother in the story (nicknamed Squirrel because of the similarity of the animal to his name). The next-eldest, Iris, has a similar personality to Anthea – 'When she had set her mind on a thing she always went straight through with it'. Rosamund ('the hopeful child') is Jane. Like their characters, the girls didn't go to school; they were mostly educated at home, although both spent a short time at the fee-paying Blackheath High School. Poor dead Fabian is the character of Robert; H.R. Millar, the illustrator of *Five Children*, drew his own son as the character of Robert who very sadly also died as a child. Just like his human compatriots, the Psammead refuses to be cast as a stereotype from Victorian literature. The name 'It' gives a clue as to his originality, as does his unusual appearance; Edith was hardly in the mood for godmothers with gossamer wings. The Psammead grumbles, enjoys flattery and reminisces about the good old days. Forget fluttering wings and shimmering gowns, the fairy emerging from the gravel pit (psammos means 'sand' in Greek) is a pretty ugly sight:

> 'Its eyes were on long horns like a snail's eyes, and it could move them in and out like telescopes; it had ears like a bat's ears, and its tubby body was shaped like a spider's and covered with thick soft fur; its legs and arms were furry too, and it had hands and feet like a monkey's.'

Edith was thrilled with Millar's interpretation of her Psammead, as he recalled:

> 'Mrs Bland was very complimentary about my illustrations and then, and many times afterwards, keenly cross-examined me as to how I did them. She was greatly intrigued by the "Psammead" itself because, as she said, it was exactly like the creature she had in her own imagination and "how did I come to imagine it too".
>
> The fact that Mrs Bland had given a clear detailed description of the animal did not satisfy her at all; she felt It must be telepathic! And it was the same through the subsequent years – culminating in such a story as *The Amulet*. She gave me no actual details of the scenes in her story, but was astonished that my pictures should illustrate what she had had in her mind. Mrs Bland forgot that she was a highly intellectual woman who could suggest in a few words events which would take some authors a whole page to describe. She had the power to suggest atmosphere, details etc without really describing them.'

Millar would always admire Edith – even though she was always late with her copy and he was left to make detailed pictures in just two or three days:

> 'There was nothing of the "popular Authoress" about Mrs Bland. For a highly intellectual woman she took the most astonishing interest in quite ordinary everyday things. She confessed that "she loved to shock people" and had the greatest dislike for 'pedestals'... there was sound basis for that "casual brilliance"

of hers. It was always so effortless – without the slightest trace of pedantry. It was this, I think, that endeared her to all and sundry.'

Millar was one of the leading illustrators of the day, and his beautiful line-drawings would continue to accompany Edith's work for fourteen years, making a significant contribution to her success.

Edith builds on the distinctive tone of voice that we first heard in *The Story of the Treasure Seekers*, as she pulls the reader aside to whisper in their ear:

> 'I could go on and make this into a most interesting story about all the ordinary things that the children did – just the kind of things you do yourself, you know... So I will only tell you the really astonishing things that happened... Grown-up people find it very difficult to believe really wonderful things, unless they have what they call proof.'

Again, Edith refuses to write about childhood with a rose-tinted pen and avoids the Victorian trend for moralising. The children's wishes never quite turn out as they hope; being as beautiful as the day leaves them homeless and starving; becoming rich results in almost being sent to prison for stealing. When they wish for wings, the children end up exhausted and on top of a church tower; and in another episode their baby brother inadvertently disappears as a result of their frustration with him.

The success of the book spawned two sequels, the first of which was *The Phoenix and the Carpet*, serialised in the *Strand Magazine* from July 1903 to June 1904. It's true that some of the details of the story seem distinctly un-PC these days (the word 'savages' probably wouldn't get past the censors had it been written today), yet Edith's imagination remains as fresh as ever, bursting from the page with sheer delight as the group of children come across a magic carpet and talking bird that takes them to exotic lands such as Babylon. What child today wouldn't be utterly captivated by the thought of their bedroom carpet whisking them around the world with a single wish? The character of the Phoenix is a more refined version of the Psammead, and provides plenty of humour.

Edith further pushed the boundaries of children's fiction in the final story of the trilogy, *The Story of the Amulet* (1906), which was the first book for young readers to explore the theme of time travel. Jane, Cyril, Anthea, Robert and the Lamb are reunited with their dear Psammead in a pet shop and take him home to live with them under the bed. They are staying near the British Museum with all its Egyptian wonders, and the trilogy is brought full circle as the Psammead's connection with the ancient civilization is revealed. Adventures include riding on woolly mammoths in the ancient city of Atlantis, helping a poor child in Roman Britain in 55BC and meeting pharaohs of ancient Egypt. The theme of time is constantly referenced by many of the characters throughout history, and Edith's Fabian utopian vision for the future is hinted at. Time applied to human life is also explored, with the many senior characters in the book depicted as wise and heroic – such as the Learned Gentleman at the crux of the story. This character was to be the first of Edith's 'important elders', echoing the Old Gentleman of *The Railway Children*, who brings the children answers just as the Learned Gentleman does. It's worth pointing out how much research Edith carried out for *Amulet*; she dedicated the book to Dr Wallis Budge of the British Museum. Known as the Keeper of Egyptian and Assyrian Antiquities, Dr Budge became Edith's lover after she boldly knocked on his door during a visit to her favourite exhibition, the Egyptian mummies (which remains one of the most popular exhibits today). Edith and Budge spent hours together working on plots inspired by Egyptian stories, magic, romance and religion, and he suggested the idea of using an amulet. As they became close, they talked sex and Edith asked him to run away with her. But while he found her physically attractive, Dr Budge wouldn't budge from his wife – he regarded Edith as a somewhat sad figure and emotionally unstable. He escaped from her on an archaeological expedition to Egypt.

With her *Five Children* trilogy, Edith had a tremendous impact on the future of children's literature. She established the rules for writing about magic that are very much followed by today's authors, as pointed out in volume three of *The Oxford Encyclopaedia of Children's Literature* by editor-in-chief Jack Zipes (Oxford University Press, 2006). To be plausible, magic must have limitations – it is only seen through certain mediums, such as when the Psammead appears for example, and limited to only three wishes. Magic doesn't always need to be explained; we accept that the amulet is a sort of time machine (in contrast, the concept is explained at great length by H.G. Wells in *The Time Machine*). That's not to say Edith didn't understand time but she chooses not to bog herself or readers down with the idea; she was clever enough to grasp the concept that time is only a mode of thought. Was she aware of relativity and the idea that all times exist simultaneously? Edith also set the notion that magic adventure doesn't take up real time; her children come back at exactly the same time as they left the amulet, and the Psammead explains that it would be wrong to mix up the present and the past. Edith explains away any communication issues in Egypt in 6000BC by saying that magic allows children to talk to and understand everyone, unlike Wells who devotes pages to his characters learning a language. Later in her career, Edith continued to write about magic for children, including

The House of Arden (1908) and *Harding's Luck* (1909) in which she ponders whether time travellers can affect history. *The Magic City* (1910) plays with the idea of a fairy tale through dimensions of fantasy and reality, *Wet Magic* (1913) features a mermaid as a magic helper and in *The Wonderful Garden* (1911, for adults), the reader is compelled to question whether the events are magical or have a rational explanation.

The Story of the Amulet had a profound effect on *The Chronicles of Narnia* author C.S. Lewis. He spoke of devouring the *Amulet* as a child growing up in Northern Ireland. 'It first opened my eyes to antiquity,' he wrote, quoting the idea of the 'dark backward and abysm of time' (taken from *Surprised by Joy* by C.S. Lewis, Geoffrey Bles, 1955). 'I can still re-read it with delight.' Rudyard Kipling, a contemporary of Edith, became one of the *Five Children* series' famous fans, and he wrote to her from South Africa in March 1903:

> 'My kiddies are five and seven (they can't read, thank goodness) and they took an interest in the Psammead stories – a profound and practical interest...
>
> 'I wish I could tell you what joy it gave them and how they revelled in the fun of it. A kiddy laughing at a joke is one of the sweetest sights under heaven and our nursery used to double up and rock with mirth. They were very indignant when the stories came to an end... they liked best the magic gold and the attempt to buy horses and carriages, and next to that the growing up of the baby...
>
> 'They [the stories] were discussed and rediscussed in all possible lights. You see we have a sandpit in our garden and there was always a chance of a Psammead!'

'Mr Kipling' is mentioned in the book for his phrase 'but that is another story'.

Kipling was impressed by Edith's ability to mix magic with the real world: '...what wasn't genuine Phoenix was genuine Camden Town and that is rare in literature.' His letters to Edith became a running joke that she caused him great trouble because her stories were so good that he had to repeatedly read them to his children. He wrote an anecdote that one of the stories in a copy of the *Strand* was fought over so much the magazine ripped and he had to hurry uphill three miles to the station to buy another:

> 'P.S If next time you publish you could run it off in a weekly it would be handier for me fetching it from the station as keeping them quieter between times.

'P.P.S The one they liked best was about the Cook and the
Burglar. Children are given to crime from youth up.'

Kipling admired Edith's work although they never met (he was notoriously
shy):

'If it isn't impertinence to say so, I've been watching your work
and seeing it settle and clarify and grow tender (this sounds like a
reviewer but it isn't) with great comfort and appreciation.'

Edith was thrilled with the positive critical reception, but, behind all the
accolades, *Five Children and It* could be read as an expression of her own
personality and her relationship with her family. Perhaps Edith drew on her
own character traits when picturing the Psammead; in her middle-age she
was described as being round and ruddy with bright, vigilant eyes that had an
expression of curiosity. Edith wasn't the traditional cuddly children's author
just as the Psammead isn't your typical fairy and in her own way, Edith was all
powerful; she understood children and spread her own particular magic as an
author. 'She could be as cantankerous as her own cantankerous Psammead, but
in all fairness it was seldom,' wrote Joan Evans Alonso, who lived at Well Hall
as a child for six years during the First World War:

'Sometimes days would pass without our seeing her. She would
be up all night writing, trying to meet some deadline. It was then
she could be ill-humoured, though not for long. John would say
"Look out, Mother is casting a gloom." And was she ever!'

Edith became known for being sharp-tongued and sarcastic, and could be
greatly tolerant or absurdly short-tempered, depending on her mood – just as the
Psammead is. Edith's first biographer, Doris Langley Moore, received widely
differing accounts about what Edith was like when she contacted her friends
and family a few years after she died. 'I am not at all surprised that all your
informants contradict each other. Impressions of E. Nesbit depended entirely
on the mood in which one met her, she had so many,' wrote one source. 'You
either loved her, or thought "that dreadful woman",' said another. 'There was
no balance in her (hence her abiding power) and she was as reliable as a water-
wagtail.' Edith's split personality expressed itself as 'Blazing inconsistencies,
her hellish and freezing tempers, her radiant warming, reviving charm'. Edith
was capable of gentle malice just as the Psammead is in his mis-granting of
wishes and she always wrote the truth just as the sand-fairy takes things literally.

Both appear eccentric and quirky, like intelligent and very clever children who enjoy adventure and absurdity. Like the Psammead, Edith had been forced to make her own way in the world. If she hadn't married Hubert and had found someone rich, perhaps she wouldn't ever have had the motivation to write.

Noël Coward met Edith in the 1920s and described her as someone who transcended time:

> 'Her moral attitude was quite genuine – I mean not attached to any fashion or period. She would have been exactly the same in the most rigid Victorian menage or the most dashing epoch of the 20th century.'

Ultimately, both the Psammead and Edith are utterly unforgettable creatures, as Joan Evans Alonso wrote:

> 'E. Nesbit had many whims. She adored flattery and loved to shock people. But though we often regarded her with awe and bewilderment, she inspired our love and affection. She liked to be embraced, and embraced us often and called us "dear".'

As another friend said of her, 'She wrote from a fund of delightful childishness of her own.'

Subconsciously or otherwise, Edith immortalised herself and her family in print with *Five Children and It*. In her forties, she had realised anew how precious life is, a sentiment particularly highlighted in a gypsy's prayer that comes when the Lamb is almost kidnapped:

> 'May he be brave, and have the strong head to think with, and the strong heart to love with, and the strong hands to work with, and the strong feet to travel with, and always come safe home to his own.'

Later, Edith reveals her constant guilt over Fabian's death when the character of Cyril says:

> '…Trying not to believe things when in your heart you are almost sure they are true, is as bad for the temper as anything I know.'

As the years went on, Edith was able to move on from escapist fantasy back to reality, bringing her readers to earth when she published a novel with a very British flavour in 1906. The book would become her most loved.

Chapter 13

The Railway Children

'I think everyone in the world is friends if you can only get them to see you don't want to be un-friends.'

The Railway Children

Arguably, no other children's novel in the English language has such a tender place in the heart of a generation than *The Railway Children*. Those who grew up watching the 1970 film adaptation starring Jenny Agutter and Bernard Cribbins will forever associate their childhood with the story of that golden summer of Edwardian England. It has been voted the third best children's film of all time.

The best of Edith Nesbit's novels, and her only non-magic children's bestseller, *The Railway Children* hasn't been out of print since it was first published in 1906 – a rare achievement for any book, let alone a children's one. It is one of the most successful children's books of that time as it continues to be frequently adapted for the stage and screen; both the plot and style of narrative transcend time in a crossover story that can still be enjoyed by adults as well as children. The book is a microcosm of Edith's beliefs about childhood, humanity, charity, class, social injustice, the goodness in people, the fact that right will come out in the end, the importance of hard work, respect of the elderly, the countryside and absent fathers.

Edith's awe of the natural world was one of the main influences on her poetry and is intrinsic to the success of *The Railway Children*, which better than any novel of its time captures the rural beauty Edwardian England. Edith always yearned for that golden England that vanished with the First World War. It was an abrupt change in direction for her from comedy-fantasy novels to realism and shows her development as a writer as she combines a gripping plot with almost faultless characterisation. Bobbie is the most likeable and fully rounded Nesbit hero, and, for the first time Edith wrote a fleshed-out adult figure in Mother. The key to the novel's enduring power is its overriding theme of the absent father, a theme Edith that had personally been dogged with throughout her life. For Edith, this loss became amalgamated with the figurative loss of her husband for she knew she could never fully possess Hubert's heart.

The Railway Children was one of three novels Edith published in 1906, along with a collection of short stories, *Man and Maid*. It was first serialised in the *London Magazine*, starting in January 1905, and the plot will be familiar to many; when their father is accused of spying, Roberta (Bobbie), Peter and Phyllis are forced to move from their red brick villa in London to the countryside to 'play at being poor for a bit' while Mother writes stories to keep food on the table. When they discover that the railway line runs close to the bottom of their garden, they become great friends with the station master, Perks, and together they witness such heroic adventures as reuniting a Russian refugee with his family, rescuing an injured schoolboy in a train tunnel, saving a baby from a fire on a barge and, most significantly, preventing a train accident after a landslide.

Edith had lived near railways all her life, and she wrote the novel at Well Hall where the railway line ran at the bottom of her garden with the station some 300m away. There is speculation about which particular train track inspired the novel. The answer might be a mixture of several, including the Kent and East Sussex Railway, between Ashford and Tenterden, near where she enjoyed holidaying at Yalding. There is an area near the railway called Three Chimneys with a farmhouse of the same name (the family's house in the book is called Three Chimneys). In the episode of the bargees when the children rescue a baby from a burning boat in the canal, the description of the bridge, pub and nineteen locks recalls the area surrounding her favourite river, the Medway in Yalding; the fictional Maidbridge could be Maidstone. Edith was also influenced by the railway line that ran at the bottom of the garden of her childhood home of Halstead Hall (although the 'Halstead for Knockholt Station' wasn't built until 1876 after she left). Another theory is that Edith was influenced by the Hope Valley line in Derbyshire, which she knew through visiting her mother and sister Saretta who lived in a cottage on the edge of the Peak District near Manchester. Whatever the exact location, it is clear the setting never strays from England (unlike her other successful children's books) and Edith drew much from her own happy childhood, and these nostalgic details lovingly shared are what makes the novel marvellously vivid; her description of the steam train shrieking and snorting and the red petticoats the children wave at the train in warning of the landslide. The plot can be traced to various incidents in her own life; Edith was friends with a Russian revolutionary, Stepniak, who inspired the episode of Shepansky. In fact, Stepniak was killed by a train in 1896. The climax when Father is finally released and Bobbie meets him at the station is heart-breaking for the double-meaning it must have had for Edith; she knew she would never,

ever see her father again: '"Oh! my Daddy, my Daddy!" That scream went like a knife into the heart of everyone in the train.' Edith would later re-write almost exactly the same lines in the climax of *The House of Arden*, which also has the long-lost father theme at the heart of the action.

The strong, intelligent and resourceful Bobbie is, arguably, the most well-drawn fictional character from children's literature of that time perhaps with the exception of Sara Crewe in *A Little Princess* by Frances Hodgson Burnett, which had been published the year before. Edith wrote 12-year-old Bobbie as the perfect daughter; a loving, modest, discreet, sensitive, capable companion who takes care of practicalities allowing her parent to write. Perhaps Edith wished Rosamund and Iris were more like Bobbie so that Alice Hoatson would be relegated from a live-in housekeeper to an occasional one, like Mrs Viney in the story. Edith wrote an improved version of herself as the character of Mother who, in the absence of Father, is forced to become the family breadwinner as a freelance writer. Mother even writes on paper with four-leafed shamrocks, Edith's lucky symbol she used as her signature. Like Bobbie, Mother is a heroine, who puts bread on to the table by writing late into the night by candlelight, soldiering on through illness while shivering under the blankets in a freezing house. When she sells a story, joy breaks loose and there are buns for tea in celebration. All these incidents are drawn from Edith's own life when, as a young mother, she kept her family afloat when Hubert went bankrupt. This Mother, however, is greatly appreciated – a sentiment Edith always felt was lacking amongst her own family and this caused a long-running argument which eventually caused her to become extremely bitter:

> '"I think it would be nice," said Bobbie, "to marry someone very poor, and then you'd do all the work and he'd love you most frightfully."'

The Old Gentleman speaks of the fictional mother as 'one in a million' and the Doctor describes Bobbie and Mother as:

> 'awfully brave... It's an odd thing – the softer and more easily hurt a woman is the better she can screw herself up to do what has to be done. I've seen some brave women – your Mother's one...'.

Edith's own mother had been a saintly sort who bravely kept calm and carried on when her husband died leaving her with five children; Edith had her in mind when she was writing the character and perhaps remembered the sorts of tender words Mrs Nesbit used when soothing her as a child such as 'chickeny love' and 'hush, then, a dear, a duck, a darling!' (also similar to the words the Bastables spoke to their baby brother the Lamb). The fact that Edith could recall such personal words suggests the very special memories that she would always treasure of her parent. Even if they weren't the exact words her mother used, maybe they were the mutterings she used to say to her own children. Edith develops these tender memories of childhood further in the sentiment that grows throughout the novel of the unbreakable love that will always lie between a mother and daughter, even after death. Mother says:

> '"No one," she said at last, "ever loved anyone more than my mother loved me."... Bobbie understood a little how people do not leave off running to their mothers when they are in trouble even when they are grown up, and she thought she knew a little what it must be to be sad, and have no mother to run to any more.'

In reality, although Edith loved her own daughters (and sons), she could have done more to cherish the bond between them. In truth, she probably spent more time writing about familial relationships than nurturing them.

Now nearing her fifties, Edith was looking deeper within herself and reflecting on her own personal history, perhaps trying to make sense of her relationship with Hubert. Mother is a character who is left with nothing at the start of the book and builds a life through sheer hard work and the strength of her humanity. Perhaps a temporary separation (or even prison sentence) is what Edith secretly wished would befall Hubert so she could establish her own life in the way she wanted it. She regularly introduced her husband to other women; did she deliberately put him into temptation's way to be shot of him? After all, that's how Hubert met Alice Hoatson, as her daughter Rosamund explains:

> 'The tragic thing was that it was E.N. who first persuaded her to go about with him in order to get him to give up another lady whom E.N. loathed. It was really rather a curious trait in her character that persisted long after she must have known the dangers of handing any girl over to him or attracting his attention to anyone. I saw it done myself when I was growing up.'

Yet whatever she really thought of her marriage, her children and her life, Edith was determined to make the best of it and live positively. '"Very wonderful and beautiful things happen, don't they? And we live most of our lives in the hope of them," says the Old Gentleman. "Stick to it," said Peter; "everything has an end, and you get to it if you only keep on." Which is quite true, if you come to think of it, and a useful thing to remember in seasons of trouble – such as measles, arithmetic, impositions, and those times when you are in disgrace, and feel as though no one would ever love you again, and you could never – never again – love anybody.'

Written more than 100 years ago, *The Railway Children* is Edith's best-known work and its heartfelt power continues to endear it to new generations. She dedicated the novel to her son, Paul, who shared with his mother his knowledge of trains to help her write accurately on the subject. Paul was Edith's favourite son, yet her relationship with him – and her other children – was becoming increasingly strained. In *The Railway Children* Edith had written the character of Mother as kind, sensible and, above everything, loving – but was the truth of Edith's life altogether different from her fiction?

Chapter 14

Five Children and E. Nesbit

'Mother... was almost always there, ready to play with the children, and read to them, and help them to do their home-lessons... she used to write stories for them... and she always made up funny pieces of poetry for their birthdays.'

The Railway Children

Edith Nesbit spent her life writing about children and their parents. Her description of the Mother character in *The Railway Children* is of a perfect Victorian angel:

'Mother did not spend all her time in paying dull calls to dull ladies, and sitting dully at home waiting for dull ladies to pay calls to her. She was almost always there, ready to play with the children, and read to them, and help them to do their home-lessons. Besides this she used to write stories for them while they were at school, and read them aloud after tea, and she always made up funny pieces of poetry for their birthdays and for other great occasions, such as the christening of the new kittens, or the refurnishing of the doll's house, or the time when they were getting over the mumps.'

Edith worked hard to maintain her public persona of a moral, benevolent authoress and made a point of replying to every fan letter, with help from Paul and her secretaries, Jimmy Horsnell and the aptly-named Charles Bastable. She genuinely enjoyed meeting her young readers and it was vital for her to stay in touch with young people to make sure her writing remained relevant. Some fans became such good pen-pals they turned into friends and received an invitation for lunch or tea at Well Hall. After the young visitors had crossed the moat to the huge door of the Tudor mansion, it would open to reveal their heroine.

Edith appeared as a sort of fairy godmother figure, peering over spectacles perched on the end of her nose as she stood tall in flowing, brown Liberty frocks with amber beads jangling and her brown curly hair pinned up messily with tortoiseshell combs. She had a knack of knowing how to put children at ease, by bringing one of her dachshunds to pat or making a joke about what was for lunch ('chicken with its boots on' – feet and all). Edith had a soft spot for children but she wasn't indiscriminate with her affection. She was kindly but sometimes aloof, and this was true amongst her own brood: she would always kiss Paul on the forehead as a queen might do – never on his cheek. Some say she was demonstrative and liked to be hugged and often blew kisses, others believed that she had something hard and shrewish about her that prevented people from becoming close to her.

Children's authors are sometimes known to be quite different in private from their public profile – famously, Enid Blyton was despised by one of her daughters. When Edith's adopted daughter Rosamund was asked by a family friend how lovely it must be to have a mother who was a children's author, she replied, 'Oh, Auntie [Alice Hoatson] was the only mother we ever knew; Mother was always too busy to attend to us.' In truth, Edith was a bohemian with a colourful romantic life. There is no question that she loved all her children and took great delight in them as babies but as they grew older, her relationship with them changed. Bringing up five children would be enough to keep most mothers occupied, even with domestic help. But Edith's unlimited energy and intellect needed to be satisfied with a life outside hearth and family. Nearly everyone who knew her said how busy she was, and the number of hobbies and activities she threw herself into is extraordinary; she was a member of the Fabian Society, and regularly raised money for the local Labour Party and underprivileged children. She took regular active holidays and was unusually sporty – she could swim well, ride a horse as well as a bike, run fast, ice skate and even high kick until she was 60. Her vigorous games of badminton on the lawn of Well Hall were legendary amongst visitors (she had a scar on her nose to prove it). Creative in all senses, Edith loved music, singing (often in French – fluently if not accurately), playing the guitar and piano; she could paint and draw well (after all, she had made her living from making greetings cards as a younger woman) and enjoyed photography, regularly taking lots of pictures of family and friends. She had a natural gift for doing anything with her hands including sewing, embroidery, dress-making and ribbon work, from which she would make kettle holders, small ornaments and a large fire screen. Much of her time was taken up with helping friends, such as mentoring young writers (which must have taken considerable thought and brainpower) and having people to stay who needed a hand. Several of her friends lived on the grounds of Well Hall such as her oldest friend Ada Breakell. As well as French she could also speak German and her enormous social circle meant her diary was a whirl of hosting parties at Well Hall; her address book bulged with names from around the world, from the ground-breaking feminist Labour MP Margaret Bondfield in Whitehall to Edward Plunkett at Dunsany Castle in Ireland, better known as Lord Dunsany, one of the greatest fantasy novelists of the day. Edith's unquenchable thirst for life and her childlike personality meant she was interested in everything she came across and was well-informed about subjects that women of the time took little interest in, such as railways and boats; the story goes that when a plumber came to Well Hall, Edith left her writing to watch him do his job and find out all about it. She even learnt brick-laying and carpentry, once making a dresser and adorning it with pokerwork, the fashionable Edwardian art of burning a pattern with a heated metal point. In addition to all this, Edith found the energy to devote to her busy professional life – she always earned more than Hubert – by the time she died she had written more than 100 published works including approximately 40 children's books, collections of poetry and stories, essays and plays, as well as public speaking engagements. She never turned work away.

It all adds up to a life in which not a minute was wasted. But did Edith sacrifice her family as a result? She always maintained that the bond between a mother and her baby is one of life's most cherished relationships and believed that holding a new baby is one of the loveliest things in the world. Throughout her life, she wrote and re-wrote about families, children, mothers and babies, and by reading between the lines of her letters, poems and novels, we can find clues to her relationship with her children. As a young mother Edith adored her infants and cherished her time with them. She wrote to her Ada Breakell about the importance of enjoying 'the little things' in domestic life:

> 'Today Hubert and I and Paul went for a walk in the country. Hubert taught Paul to climb stiles, an accomplishment of which he (Paul) is very proud... Paul has cut his leg and had to have it sewn up. It was rather fearful for him, poor little chap... Paul is now learning to read...'

When Hubert went bankrupt and Edith was quickly forced to be the breadwinner for her young family, she drew upon what she knew to write her potboilers for magazines – and the poems and stories she produced at this time are often tender tales of young motherhood such as 'The Star', from *Lays and Legends* (Longmans, Green & Co, 1886). One of her greatest sympathies as a socialist was with mothers on the breadline, as the poem shows:

> 'This is my baby, it came to me,
> Washed ashore by a magic sea
> Where I floated veiled in the foam of dreams
> Others walked on a path of schemes,
> Money, position paved the way;
> They never knew a day like my day
>
> There was no present, there was no past
> Nothing had lasted, nothing could last,
> Nothing mattered but one gold star.
> And here my little one, here you are,
> Star of the shepherds, star of the wise
> And the workhouse infirmary saw it rise.'

As Edith became an established writer and turned her hand to novels, babies featured regularly in her children's books – from the Lamb in *Five Children and It*, to the baby on the barge that Roberta rescues in *The Railway Children*. All these infants are regarded as one of life's most precious gifts. Her dedication of *Five Children and It* in 1902 to her son John, the real Lamb, shows the tenderness of her love for children and still resonates with anyone who feels babies grow up too quickly:

> 'My Lamb, you are so very small,
> You have not learned to read at all.
> Yet never a printed book withstands
> The urgence of your dimpled hands.
> So, though this book is for yourself,
> Let mother keep it on the shelf
> Till you can read. O days that pass,
> That day will come too soon, alas!'

As her babies grew into children, Edith allowed them the freedom to enjoy exactly the sorts of adventures she wrote about as they roamed the streets of Lewisham and, later, the grounds of Well Hall; playing in the moat and making pocket money by selling wildflowers to commuters at the station. Unusually for late Victorian/early Edwardian children, there weren't many rules aside from learning their grammar, being polite and never being late for dinner; occasional smacks and being sent to bed early were their punishments. The children weren't spoilt with limitless toys and instead encouraged to enjoy the company of the house's constant stream of fascinatingly wonderful adult visitors. 'One need not always "talk down" to children: they understand far better than you think,' wrote Edith in *Wings and the Child or The Building of Magic Cities* (1913), her non-fiction culmination of a lifetime of thinking about children. In it she discusses why the freedom to explore and play is essential for childhood development and some of her points read as a modern parenting manual. Edith was part of a movement that was sweeping away the old Victorian tradition that children should be seen and not heard: to put it into context, Robert Baden-Powell's Scout Movement had been established for several years and already had more than 100,000 members. One of the key points Edith gets across in *Wings and the Child* is that children should be allowed their freedom:

'Liberty is one of the rights that a child above all needs – every possible liberty, of thought, of word, of deed.'

Edith's own childhood had been remarkably free, romping across Europe and running wild in the Kent countryside, and as a parent, Edith, together with Hubert, moved their young family from London to the countryside to encourage a love of the outdoors. She was committed to the notion of learning through play and eschewed buying her children countless toys and instead showed them how to make building blocks with household objects as she believed it developed their imagination, taught patience and perseverance and helps children keep their temper (because no one can build in a rage). In *Wings and the Child* Edith doesn't hide her distrust of consumerism, warning against buying too many toys especially ones that don't encourage the imagination. Nature is an excellent plaything she believed, writing that children never tire of mud, shells, sticks and stones – still true today. Sand in particular will always be a favourite, she wrote, because there is so much of it and it is malleable. Beaches and sandpits across the world would agree.

Yet strangely, as her children grew up, Edith reduced their freedoms. She was frank (and responsible) enough to talk to her children about the facts of life, something many parents felt was unmentionable but a subject Edith felt was important to be discussed openly. 'If your child has learned to love and trust you it will come to you with its questions', she wrote. But it seems she didn't trust her own children and Hubert was famously protective of his girls, refusing to allow them to be unconventional. Edith read their personal letters, made friends with their friends and had strict rules on boyfriends. When Iris was at the Slade art school she met a creative bunch, including Berta Ruck who became one of Edith's good friends; she would become a celebrated author, whose name perhaps inspired the character of Roberta in *The Railway Children*. Although it is natural that a parent should take an interest in her daughter's friends, it could have been smothering for Iris to have a domineering Edith joining in her social circle and inviting her chums on holiday. When the girls were older, Edith caused a nuisance when she tried to butt in on Iris' love affairs and she and Rosamund were hurt that she read their letters. They both had chaperones and there was an incident when 14-year-old Iris wasn't allowed to bring along a platonic male friend to a music concert at Queen's Hall in London. More seriously, Hubert was accused of seducing one of Rosamund's school friends. He would later write of a father's sexual possessiveness in his essay *Letters to a Daughter* in 1906 (Michael Kennerley).

In her early fifties, Edith published a collection of short stories about the unbreakable bond between a mother and child, inspired by her relationship with her own mother as well as her experience of motherhood. *These Little Ones* features a tale called 'The Three Mothers', which describes a well-to-do mother who lost her baby and can never forgive herself for it, just as Edith always blamed herself for the death of Fabian. *These Little Ones* is dedicated to Alice Hoatson. Was this dedication meant to out Alice as a single mother, an attempt by Edith to gain acknowledgement for having adopted the two children her housekeeper had borne after sleeping with Hubert? Edith's view of motherhood and her relationship with her five children were inextricably bound up with the figure of Alice, who was both a help and hindrance. Without the Mouse as nanny and housekeeper, Edith couldn't have become a successful novelist. But Alice's loyalty to the family meant that she was a constant presence at Well Hall, a temptation for Hubert and an indelible reminder to Edith of his unfaithfulness. It wore away at Edith, as did the sadness of lost motherhood; after all, Edith had buried Fabian and her stillborn baby and suffered at least two miscarriages. She developed horrendous mood swings and could be as furious as a gathering thunder-cloud and flash into a prima donna's rage, as one friend remembered:

> 'Having spread panic, blight and depression over the entire household of which one member had displeased her, she would withdraw behind an emphatically-closed door, and there stay, leaving those who loved her to the darkness. When she emerged – a sunburst! The entire landscape and population

would bask in that genial all-pervading warmth, charm and sympathy that streamed from her...'

Iris remembered that it was Hubert who was constantly called upon to bring her round:

> '...he was absolutely the only person who had any influence on her moods and who could control her tantrums and bring her round to reason. And he took a lot of trouble to do it too, though it often brought on a heart attack and then of course she was overwhelmed with contrition and full of tenderness for him.'

By the time her children had grown up, it seemed Edith had not and her relationship with them soured.

Paul, her eldest, became a stockbroker in the City although apparently not a very good one. Of her sons, Edith was the closest to him and he lived at home with her until he was 37; they had similar personalities in the way that they were both daydreamers but Paul failed to inherit any of Edith's practicality. His gentleness enraged Hubert who was always disappointed in his son's lack of career success and frustrated because of their very different personalities. Some called Paul sullen and sad, others a lacklustre loner, but his sister Iris believed that he was simply on a different wavelength and family disagreements would go over his head. Iris' friend, Berta Ruck, described him as 'mild and distracted... such a trial to his father'. Apparently, Hubert once asked her if Paul had ever tried to kiss her. When she said no, Hubert said, 'I thought as much. I don't believe there is any hope for him.' Berta describes Paul as somewhat of a misfit: '[he was] a little overawed by the society that filled the house. (I know he used to walk me to the other end of Kent to get away from it).' Paul was a fair and gentle baby, and Edith joked that he should have been a girl and Iris a boy because he was less determined than she; Paul would ask for help rather than be brave enough to try new things for himself. Perhaps Edith's maternal instinct felt protective of him as he was never as healthy and strong as his siblings after suffering typhoid as a child; as an older man he was knocked back by acute bronchitis. Thoughtful and affectionate, Paul always remained close to his mother, acting as her secretary and patiently writing many letters on her behalf. In turn, Edith respected him as a confidante in important matters.

Iris was close in age to Paul, born the following year after his birthday. Naughty as a child and fiercely independent, she was her mother's favourite and Edith would show her more affection and confide in her more than the others. Iris hated her father throughout her childhood, and as an adult never could bring herself to see him in a favourable light. She thought her mother was a saint for putting up with his affairs, and respected and admired her for keeping the family afloat in the early years of her writing. But she wasn't above seeing her mother's melodramatic faults (of which she said Edith was unaware):

> '...my mother was never really interested in girls, or in women
> for that matter. She herself, as a child, was more like a boy. She
> just didn't understand girls at all.'

Iris' view contradicts Edith's own perception of herself who believed her success as a writer was precisely because she could understand young people thanks to her 'persistent and imperishable' memory. Iris inherited her mother's talent for drawing and painting, and was good enough to get into the prestigious Slade School of Fine Art. But she didn't seem to pick up her mother's spirit of optimism and was quite a downbeat person until she had a baby in 1908 with her new husband, Austin Philips, six years her senior – a civil servant from Manchester who became a novelist thanks to a little help from his mother-in-law. They married on 5 February 1907 and Iris moved back to Well Hall the year after to have her baby. Despite being ill for several weeks after the birth, Iris doted on her healthy little Pandora who gave her a focus for happiness in her life, as Edith once wrote, 'She has something to love now. The adored child, Pandora takes all her time and energy and fills her life.' The birth brought Iris close to Rosamund, who helped nurse her back to health; indeed, Pandora was originally going to be named after her aunt.

Of all her children, Edith's adopted daughter Rosamund was the most similar to her – on paper at least. As extroverts, they loved showing off, and were both beauties who were greatly admired and enjoyed plenty of flirting and love affairs. Rosamund was the only one of Edith's children who would go on to be published; a novel of her own in 1934 called *The Man in the Stone House*. Previously, in 1925, she had edited a collection of Edith's short stories. Rosamund resembled Hubert with her dark eyes and short resolute profile but didn't look dissimilar to her mother – none of the children did (conveniently, as Rosamund once joked). Like her adopted mother, she went on to marry a journalist who was also a socialist. But Rosamund thought Edith was a Jekyll-and-Hyde-character – thoroughly loveable, kind and generous but prone to horrendous tantrums that regularly ruined mealtimes.

Edith didn't seem to feel the same resentment towards her other adopted child, John, who was the most academic of the family although she was irked about Hubert's disproportionate pride over John's fine brain. As a teenager, John got into the prestigious City of London School to study Classics and he was a harsh critic of his mother's work especially the instructional parts of her stories.

Each of Edith's four living children was caught under the domineering influence of an overbearing mother. As an adult, Iris described her memories of Edith's volatile personality:

> 'There would be a steamy scene at meals ending in a hysterical outburst, when she would rush from the table and retired into her study with a violent slam of the door, leaving a shattered family staring uncomfortably at their pudding plates. Daddy would say "Oh, God!" and make for his study, also slamming the door. But always after a short while one would hear him going up to her room and beg to be let in. She would open the door and one could hear a murmur of affectionate phrases "Now Cat dearest, don't go on like that. Your old Cat loves you and you love your poor old Cat, don't you? There, kiss your old Cat and come and have your pudding." And so on. He comforted her and cajoled her and he always stuck by her and excused her to us however unreasonable and fiendish she had been. And more often than not they would come down the stairs arm in arm and she would kiss us all round and eat her pudding.'

Iris believed her father to be 'very dominant', having a 'tremendous hold' on Edith 'from the moment he met her until he died'. As for the ménage a trois that continued with Alice, Iris explains how Edith would have preferred to share Hubert with Alice than not have him at all, and says that her mother would put up with a great deal from anyone who gave her affection, especially her husband:

> 'It wasn't simply that he came up nobly to scratch over a big crisis. She could not have borne losing him and there was a danger of that. He didn't want to lose either of them and I've no doubt he used every art of which he was capable to keep them both. And through a lifetime of riots and jealousies he succeeded.'

Edith was capable of huge gestures but also great selfishness; because she had performed a noble act by adopting John and Rosamund, she thought this excused her erratic behaviour. Hubert exacerbated it by being affectionate to Rosamund and John but indifferent to Iris and disliking Paul. Rosamund explained what it was like growing up with E. Nesbit as a mother:

'The real truth is that everyone had a great deal to put up with from everyone else… I know that all parents are apt to stress their sacrifices to their offspring and to bemoan the lack of gratitude they receive but I assure you that, from my earliest days to my escape from home, I had that dinned into me day after day. She never let me off and she had all her early generosity to justify the demands. Gratitude was a word thrown at my head and my mother's head [Alice] and my father's head for years and I'm afraid everyone got a bit sick of it even when it was justified.'

We can see, then, that Edith's fictional mother and child relationships were different from her real-life ones. Her pent-up resentment began to wear away at her face, figure and frayed nerves; as her thin lips became more hard-set, she began to put on weight elsewhere and lose her slim figure. She once complained to a friend, 'Water runs downhill. The affection you get back from children is sixpence given as change for a sovereign.' Edith's success as a children's author was through her great understanding of children – a result of her exceptional memory rather than a deep maternal instinct. Ultimately, her childlike personality meant she wasn't suited to the role of parent. She wrote of the 'great gulf' between one generation and another, and this became sadly true of her own family as she grew apart from them:

'You cannot hope to understand a child by common-sense, by reason, by logic, nor by any science whatsoever. You cannot understand them by imagination – not even by love itself. There is only one way: to remember what you thought and felt and liked and hated when you yourself were a child. Not what you know now – or you think you know – you ought to have thought and liked, but what you did then, in stark fact, like and think. There is no other way.'

Chapter 15

Edith and H.G. Wells

'Every self-respecting family will buy you automatically and you will be rich beyond the dreams of avarice, and I knock my forehead on the ground at your feet in the vigour of my admiration of your easy artistry.'

H.G. Wells in a letter to Edith [1]

In 1908 H.G. Wells stood on the smoky platform of Paddington railway station and put his hand protectively on the shoulder of 21-year-old Rosamund Bland, who was dressed in disguise as a boy. Despite twenty years between them and Wells being married to his second wife, the couple were in the throes of a thrilling affair and eloping to Paris in secret. As they boarded the train, a tall, dark shape came running along the platform, hurriedly glancing into every window as he passed. It was Hubert Bland, and when he spotted his daughter with Wells, he hauled the 41-year-old off the train, threatened him with public scandal and smartly punched him. At Hubert's side was the lovestruck Clifford Sharp, a fellow political journalist and Fabian who proposed to Rosamund shortly afterwards.

This outrageous story fuelled the rumour mill for years, although the exact details have never been uncovered. Wells did admit to a love affair with Rosamund, describing it as:

'a steamy, jungle episode, a phase of coveting and imitative desire, for I never found any great charm in Rosamund. I would rather I had not to tell of it.' [2]

As the founder of modern science fiction, Herbert George Wells was one of the greatest writers, journalists and thinkers of the early twentieth century. He was an advocate of free love and his startling blue eyes and trademark moustache along with his fine brain and gift of conversation made him irresistible to women, earning him the self-styled reputation as a Don Juan among the intelligentsia. He once wrote:

'I have done what I pleased, so that every bit of sexual impulse in me has expressed itself. I am a very immoral person. I have preyed on people who loved me.'

Edith had met him in 1902 through the Fabian Society and became very close to him, although it is not known if they were intimate. They had plenty in common, as they loved spending time with young people, were both incredibly generous and loved socialising, debates and long walks. Each grew up in south-east London and Kent, had holiday homes near each other and even shared a secretary, Jimmy Horsnell. Wells described Edith as 'a tall, whimsical, restless, able woman who had been very beautiful and was still very good-looking...' He liked visiting Edith and family, describing Well Hall as 'extraordinarily open and jolly' and a place to play badminton and 'gossip and discuss endlessly'. He dropped in unannounced one July on the 'easy Bohemian household' to finish a draft of his novel *In the Days of the Comet* (1906). Edith welcomed him warmly and he stayed for a week; the pair would talk well into the night and into the early hours. Famous for his prolific and entertaining correspondence, Wells wrote to Edith to thank her for the 'bright dear time', stating how he left home broken and returned fixed and inspired:

'a yellow, embittered and thoroughly damned man on one Thursday and his return on the next, pink... exultant... full of the most agreeable memories. If – as I have always said – the gratitude of a lifetime...'

Wells was always complimentary about Edith's work and believed it was underrated, writing this later dated from 1904:

'Steamed Lady
'I never told you how we like the *Phoenix and the Carpet* and how extraordinarily more than the late Mrs Ewing who was once first we now esteem you. The Phoenix is a great creation; he is the best character you ever invented – or anybody ever invented in this line. It is the best larking I ever saw. Your destiny is plain. You go on every Xmas never missing a Xmas, with a book like this, and you will become a British Institution in six years from now. Nothing can stop it. Every self-respecting family will buy you automatically and you will be rich beyond the dreams of avarice, and I knock my forehead on the ground at your feet in the vigour of my admiration of your easy artistry.'

He nicknamed Edith 'Ernest' as there was a running joke between them that when he first read her novels, he thought she was a man and her initial 'E' stood for Ernest. 'Ernest' in turn repaid his compliment by mentioning her friend in the sequel to *The Phoenix and the Carpet*. Wells appears as the 'great reformer' in the utopian vision of the future in Chapter 12 of *The Story of the Amulet*:

> "'Why do you call him 'Wells'?" asked Robert, as the boy ran off.
> "'It's after the great reformer – surely you've heard of him? He
> lived in the dark ages, and he saw that what you ought to do is to
> find out what you want and then try to get it. Up to then people
> had always tried to tinker up what they'd got.'"

Their close friendship, both professionally and personally, led Edith to ask Wells to support Rosamund's fledgling attempts at writing – a somewhat ironic request when read in retrospect after the scandal between the pair:

> 'Don't, please, discourage Rosamund. She must earn her living.
> If Hubert or I were to die she'd have to earn it at once: I want her
> to be able to earn it by writing and not have to go into a shop, or
> be a humble companion.'

In another letter Edith professed to Wells, 'We do love you so very much', and the writers built a mutual respect for each other's work, sharing the idea of time travel as a central theme in their novels.

Wells had also become great friends with Hubert through their political passion, although after three years of working alongside each other in the Fabian Society, Wells began to tire of it. Describing himself as a democratic socialist, he criticised the Society in 1906 with his paper *The Faults of the Fabian*. He believed it must be reformed 'inside out and then throw it in the dustbin' – in his eyes it had become a municipal club run by an old boys' gang for twenty years. He believed that to make real change, the Society needed to attract many more members and become overtly political. He held a debate with George Bernard Shaw but lost, and eventually resigned his membership. Wells continued his friendship with the Blands but their relationship began to sour as he learnt more about the family:

> 'At first it seemed to be a simple agreeable multitudinousness from
> which literary buds and flowers sprang abundantly, presided over
> by this tall, engaging, restless, moody, humorous woman. Then

gradually the visitor began to perceive at first unsuspected trends and threads of relationship and scented, as if from the moat, a more disturbing flavour. People came to Well Hall and went, and some of them went for good. There had been "misunderstandings".

'I thought at first that Well Hall was a new group for us and now in the retrospect I realise that it was a new sort of world. It was a world of rôle and not of realities.'[2]

Wells distrusted Hubert's 'man of the world' persona, insincere politics and morals and believed that he had unnatural feelings for Rosamund:

'In that hothouse atmosphere of the Bland household at Dymchurch and Well Hall... I found myself almost assigned as the peculiar interest of Rosamund, the dark-eyed sturdy daughter of Bland and the governess, Miss Hoatson. Rosamund talked of love, and how her father's attentions to her were becoming unfatherly. I conceived a great disapproval of incest, and an urgent desire to put Rosamund beyond the reach in the most effective manner possible, by absorbing her myself.'

He described Hubert as craving illicit relations with his daughter and became close to Rosamund, resulting in the Paddington train station incident that severed his relationship with the Blands forever. After the scandal, Hubert felt Wells had turned his daughter against him – Rosamund had called her father a 'fearful rogue' for lecturing her on having an affair when his own morality was so shabby. In turn, Wells never forgave Hubert and felt bitterness towards him for the rest of his life – more than twenty years later he wrote scathingly about the Blands in his book *Experiments in Biography* published in 1934, and also in *The New Machiavelli* (1910), which wasn't published for fear of libel. Wells openly criticised their marriage and accused Hubert of feeling insecure about having a successful wife. 'The two of them dramatised life and I had as yet met few people who did that. They loved scenes and "situations".' He teased Edith for 'her wit and freaks and fantasies'. Their mutual friend George Bernard Shaw at first tried to reconcile the two men but Wells sharply told him where to get off, resulting in an amusing war of the words between the two intellectuals.

Rosamund Bland married Clifford Dyce Sharp the year after the Paddington scandal in September 1909; they had known each other for years as junior Fabians, in a group nicknamed the Fabian Nursery. He had read engineering at University College, London but failed his degree as he wanted to be a journalist;

he eventually became the first editor of the *New Statesman* which was set up in 1913 by members of the Fabians including Beatrice and Sidney Webb.

In the meantime, Wells began another of his affairs with a young Cambridge graduate from the Fabian Society and got her pregnant. Edith and Rosamund were both disappointed not to have Wells in their life anymore – Edith wrote to him imploring: 'Don't you think there ought to be a time-limit for quarrels?' Perhaps Rosamund never stopped loving him, as years later she dedicated *The Man in the Stone House* to him; it was set in Romney Marsh, near where he lived in Sandgate. Her last letter to him still hints at the fondness she kept in her heart for her former lover:

> 'Clifford came home the other night and thrust a page of *The Tatler* under my nose, saying "There's HG for you." And it really was! You cannot imagine how glad I was to see him again...
>
> 'This was once my HG and I think in some deep place in me is still my HG...I re-read your earlier books – all that I read at nineteen and twenty. I found then that what I had, for years, thought of as "Rosamund" was simply something made up of bits of HG Wells. It was a shock to find there was no "I" at all, that thoughts and feelings that I had supposed my own were all to be found in you.' [3]

The Bland family's epic row with H.G. Wells became the stuff of family myth and shook Well Hall to its foundations. Yet the relationship Wells had developed with Edith would inspire her to explore the ideas of a socialist utopia. At the same time that he was writing *The Invisible Man* and *The Time Machine*, Edith was working on her own time-travelling adventure, called *The Magic City* (1910).

Chapter 16

Utopia

'I have undertaken to build a 'magic city' of bricks and dominos and odds and ends, at Olympia for the Children's Welfare Exhibition.'

Edith in a letter to her brother, Harry

Now 55 years old, Hubert Bland lay in bed, weak and almost blind, having just heard the devastating news from his doctor that his sight could never be recovered. He had always been very short-sighted in one eye (his monocle had a practical function as well as fashionable one) but it is thought that he lost the use of his other eye after a fall caused the retina to become detached. Worse, he had suffered a heart attack in November 1910 after years of chronic heart problems and the doctor had told him it was unlikely he would ever regain his health. Hubert was prone to bouts of melancholy and felt the blow keenly; he once wrote 'intelligence is only increased capacity for pain', and, 'if pessimism is sure, practically, to be wrong, unmitigated optimism is by no means certain, practically, to be right.' Yet as he lay in bed, his world growing dimmer, he resolved to face blindness bravely and not complain. He was determined to bear it like a man with a cheerful outlook and continue to work as best he could. Hubert was prescribed complete rest, and after a month by the sea in Looe, Cornwall, he resigned as honorary treasurer from the Fabian Society after twenty-seven years of service and gave up lecturing. But he managed to continue his famous weekly column for the *Sunday Chronicle* by dictating his words to Alice, who was spending an increasing amount of time with him – much to Edith's irritation. Now that Alice wasn't required to look after the children, she adopted a new role as Hubert's secretary, reading to him so he could write his weekly book reviews for the *New Statesman*, of which his son-in-law Clifford Sharp, was editor.

Hubert had always earned less than his wife but his newly reduced income had an impact on the family finances, which were not looking healthy. Edith had lost time and money on a failed venture, *The Neolith,* a magazine that she edited in 1907. She was one of a number of female editors of the period; Rachel Beer was editor of the *Sunday Times* from the mid-1890s until 1901, and then took on the role at the *Observer* until 1904. You can just imagine how such an exciting new project would have thrilled Edith, as someone who lived by instinct and acted on impulse. Working with her were her wordsmith friends and acquaintances Everest Jackson, Graily Hewitt and Spencer Pryse who all invested £10 in the project. Edith called upon all her literary chums to contribute and had an impressive list of freelancers including George Bernard Shaw, Oswald Barron, Laurence Housman and Lord Dunsany. The latter was always grateful to her for his big break. The editorial team was keen to offer readers a different sort of magazine than was currently on the market, and the publication could be said to be an extension of Edith's personality – she wanted to live her life beautifully and truthfully, and encouraged her writers to submit work in this vein:

> 'You may say exactly what you like. It seems possible that there may be something that you want to say, something that you would not easily place in a Harmsworth or Pearson publication. I want all the literary contributions to be in the most beautiful English and they may be as plain spoken as they will.'

It was Graily Hewitt's job to copy out the journalists' words into beautiful handwriting, not easy when Edith kept missing deadlines. 'It was rather a harassing time for me… we were always behind…' Yet Edith's charm overcame her disorganisation and the pair were friends – Hewitt eventually became a novelist so they had lots to talk about – and he was invited to Well Hall where she encouraged him with his work as she did with so many other young writers. 'To me she was always kindness itself,' said Hewitt:

> 'She struck me as an extraordinarily generous-hearted woman, unbusinesslike by nature, yet scrambling through somehow. She told me once of a serial she was contracted to write for some magazine, her first chapters being due in a day or two. And she hadn't begun to write anything…. "I'll write a non-committal chapter or two in an hour or two".'

Edith was famous for being able to concentrate and write unconcernedly in the middle of a crowd, smoking like a chimney all the while.

Although Edith always loved the countryside rather than the city, for *The Neolith* project she rented a London pied à terre for a year in the heart of the theatre district over the Royal Theatre at Royalty Chambers in Dean Street, Soho. The building appears in her 1911 novel, *Dormant,* where she describes an office tucked away between the box office and the entrance to the pit seats. Inside there are the type of higgledy-piggledy bohemian furnishings that Edith felt so comfortable with, such as mismatching furniture including an oak church table as a desk, comfy chairs, a mug with flowers in, a Persian carpet, Indian matting and a dishevelled leopard-skin chaise longue. After years of living in the country, Edith threw herself back into the London scene, eating exotic takeaway dinners from small local shops and having dinner in Soho, linking up with her fun and fabulous friends such as Cecil Chesterton and Gerald Gould. Young people made her feel youthful and she drank in their ideas and zest for life. Although she was confident in herself, she was always ready to listen to fresh ideas and adopt them into her way of thinking. As Wells described her, 'She was a woman who hatched a brood of novelists in much the same way as a hen hatches chickens.' While some of the writers she had acted as patroness for hadn't achieved greatness, several of her former lovers had now become established in the literary scene, with Chesterton as a leading journalist of the day and Gould as a poet. She adored hosting her young friends after dinner at her flat, where they'd play charades over coffee and beer. Edith would tinkle on the piano, her wild curly hair coming unpinned as she sang along to songs such as *Rolling Down the Medway* and sea shanties. Although oh-so unconventional, Edith was a stickler for manners and would be furious with people who were late. The story goes that at a particular Royalty Chambers dinner party, one guest was so late Edith and friends were about to tuck in to second helpings. As she heard him arrive, Edith meanly scooped up all the dinners into a casserole dish and churlishly hid it from him! She met new friends through the magazine, including W.B. Yeats and another person who was very different in background, profession and age to her but one who would become a friend for the rest of her life and who would always speak well of her. Edward Andrade was a notable physics professor at the University of London who submitted poetry to *The Neolith* – although his work was never published, they always remained good friends. At the magazine's launch party, the team had dinner in Soho at a place called Villa Villa, after which Edith hosted an after-party at her flat, borrowing the restaurant owner's guitar in exchange for an invitation.

The Neolith ran for four issues before it folded due to high production costs and low readership. Despite this, Edith relished the experience and remained associated with periodicals for most of her life – like many writers such as Charles Dickens, Thomas Hardy and George Eliot, it was how she got her big break and magazines were the first place her most famous stories were published before being turned into books.

Edith's junket at *The Neolith* added to the family's financial misfortune. For three years, the Blands had been racking up expenses from running three houses – Well Hall, the London flat at Royalty Chambers in Dean Street (later moving to 42, Rathbone Place once the lease ran out), and a holiday home in Dymchurch. Edith gave up the latter but couldn't bear not to have a place by the sea and so replaced it with another rented cottage, a former smuggler's den called Crowlink, on the cliffs above the Seven Sisters in West Sussex. Ever superstitious, she nailed charms all over the doors to keep ghosts away and was inspired to keep writing as she gazed out of the dormer windows over the coast at East Dene. She used the place as a bolt-hole to write away from Well Hall, where she was becoming increasingly resentful of her children who were spending less and less time with her.

Although Edith's bohemian attitude placed scant value on money, she knew enough that she had to write hard to bankroll her lifestyle and in 1911 published *The Wonderful Garden* for children and *Dormant*, an adult novel with a mix of magic and realism. The latter was popular enough to be published in the United States under the name *Rose Royal*. Edith hadn't had a good track record with her publishers – unusually, her books were published by lots of different companies as she didn't trust them enough to be loyal. She wasn't precious about her work ('I am not thin-skinned about my fiction') but argued fiercely over payments. Edith looked back bitterly at how little financial reward she believed she had been given for her successful novels. She sold outright the copyright of all the work she did for the publisher Raphael Tuck – although she got wise to this and didn't do so for any other publisher. She demanded handsome advances on royalties such as £200 for *Salome and the Head*, which was written in just thirty days in 1909. She said her most profitable work turned out to be the *Baby Seed Song*, which was set to music and still appears as a lullaby in modern collections today. But the Bland family suffered a loss of some £500 in 1912, when, for the first time in ten years, the *Strand Magazine* didn't publish one of her serials. Edith was bitterly disappointed and blamed her agent for being careless, as she told her brother Harry in a letter:

> 'It was a great blow to me when, owing to the muddle-headedness
> of an agent, *The Strand* did without me… It made me very hard
> up, and added considerably to the worry of life.'

These letters to her brother were a great pleasure in Edith's life – an inexpensive one, and although she hadn't seen Harry for some twenty-five years since he left for Australia, they would always write warmly and she would send him copies of her books and ask him for ideas for plots. He too was a writer and set up a newspaper in Brisbane. Edith enjoyed contributing to it, offering him an unpublished poem, quite a scoop for a new publication. When Edith sent him a copy of *The Magic City* in 1910 her letter was downbeat:

> 'I have no good news this time. Hubert's eyes have gone wrong –
> at least one of them has, and the doctors fear he may lose the sight
> of it altogether. But there is still hope. I wish things would turn
> out so that you could come back to England.'

In spring 1912 he wrote to ask if she could invest in his newspaper but she didn't even have the spare cash for that: 'we are awfully hard up at present… but I will send you a poem which you can use if you like. It has not been published.' The light-heartedness of life was fading for Edith; after thirty years of writing, she was still the main breadwinner, still in debt and, as she neared retirement age, it was wearing her down. Perhaps she felt resentful towards the friends she had been so generous to over her lifetime who were now successful but not doing more to help her in her hour of need. Fortunately, Bernard Shaw lent the Blands some money to tide them over.

Eventually, Edith was given an unusual opportunity to make some much-needed cash. Today's authors are obliged to have a public face in order to sell their books; to go on tour, speak at book festivals and answer questions on television and radio. Books are sometimes published on the strength of the possibility of their being made into a television series or film. It is testament to Edith's pull as a celebrity of the day that in 1912 she was one of the first authors to experiment with the concept of brand extension. *The Magic City* is based on a game she used to play with Paul of building tiny cities from cardboard boxes and other household objects. When sales figures showed the novel wasn't selling well, Edith asked her publisher, Macmillan, whether she could attempt to shift more copies by bringing the book to life and proposed building a real miniature city at the world-famous department store, Selfridges. Off Edith marched down Oxford Street to meet its founder, the pioneering American retailer Harry Selfridge. No doubt amused by the formidable author's enthusiastic suggestion, the innovative entrepreneur agreed. After all, he was known for his clever marketing ideas and often held book readings in his grand London store. But the story goes that Edith used so many bricks from the toy department that the manager refused to give her any more and she stormed out in frustration. Attempting to try again in other department stores, such as Hamleys and Debenhams, was discussed but in the end Edith came up with hosting an event on a grander scale at the Children's Welfare Exhibition at Olympia in London. She was delighted at having such amusement to occupy her – perhaps she found it cathartic to create a hopeful, shining new world when her own wasn't much fun – although later in a letter to her brother Harry admitted she underestimated how much work it would all take:

> 'I have undertaken to build a "magic city" of bricks and dominos and odds and ends, at Olympia for the Children's Welfare Exhibition. And in order that it may be advertised beforehand I have had to build a part of it – about 10ft x 6, in the flat which I share with Iris (she does dressmaking). The bit of the city which I have built looks jolly nice, but it is a most awful fag to do. I will try to send photographs of it when they come out. I am to have a stand 32ft x 20, which will be like a room, open on one side and lining with blue (to show like sky), Millar's illustrations are also to be shown. The tables on which the city will be built will be about 18ft by 8 so you can see it's no light job, to cover all that space with towers and bridges and palaces and gardens, all made of common objects of the house, such as biscuit tins and bowls and chessman and draughts, of dominos and tea-kettle lids…
>
> 'I had no idea when I undertook this Magic City building what a bother it would be, or I should never have undertaken it – but they say it will be a very good advertisement. I am also to read fairy tales aloud at Olympia.'

When exhibition day finally came, all the hard work was worth it and Edith loved basking in the praise from her adoring fans. Although a bit of a battleaxe these days (she argued with her publisher over money and complained she wasn't being promoted enough), she adored the camaraderie amongst her fellow stallholders and the drama of finishing her magic city in time. It's easy to imagine her pulling in everyone to help at the last minute, as she recalls fondly in her non-fiction book *Wings and the Child or The Building of Magic Cities*, which she wrote the year after the exhibition. Edith's magic city project lasted beyond the walls of Olympia. Friends who visited her at Well Hall often saw her making her beloved constructions and children were always invited to join in. But after the poor sales of *The Magic City*, there were whispers that she was becoming unpopular – possibly because the book vents Edith's opposition to votes for women, mocking suffragettes, suggesting they are aggressive and unfeminine. Edith's publishers began to feel she was out of touch with what children wanted to read and at 54 she wrote her very last children's book, *Wet Magic*, serialised in the *Strand Magazine* from December 1912 to August 1913. Edith would never work for the publication again, despite her decade of connection with it. Perhaps Edith began to lose confidence as she started to slow down in late middle age. She wrote to Harry:

'Things are pretty black for us – Hubert has practically lost his sight – he is undergoing a very expensive treatment which may do some good, but so far has done very little, if any. I am getting very tired of work, and the expenses of life don't seem to get less. I wish everyone had a small pension at 50 – enough to live on. I have had a novel in hand for some time, but I have been too worried to get on with it.'

Edith's magic cities were left scattered, abandoned and gathering dust in the attic and she began to build more sinister creations, ugly buildings that she would set fire to in the garden at Well Hall in protest of industrialisation, an issue that had concerned her and Hubert all their lives. Ironically, considering their socialist views, Hubert and Edith disliked the workers' estate that was being built on the other side of Well Hall Road and objected to the 'caterpillars' (shops and houses) destroying the age-old rural beauty of Eltham. The farmland surrounding the house had started being developed a year after Edith and her family moved there, and by 1905 the country lane had become the main road to Woolwich with trams passing through from Woolwich to Eltham from 1910. When she was 51, Edith had devoted a novel to a protest against industrialisation, *Harding's Luck* (Hodder & Stoughton 1909), about Dickie Harding, an Oliver-Twist-type character from Deptford, based on the children Edith hosted Christmas parties for as a young mother. The orphan is given the opportunity of a new life in the countryside (with a little help from time-travelling magic). Written as a novel rather than a serial for magazines, it is a sort of sequel to *The House of Arden* (1908), about two children who are eventually reunited with their father and their family's fortunes. It can be read as a fictional companion to *Wings and the Child or The Building of Magic Cities*. In both, Edith argues passionately for the importance of education and implores the government to improve the quality of schools by spending less on prisons. In *Harding's Luck*, the hero is ultimately rewarded when he sacrifices personal wealth and title in exchange for familial comforts:

'It was the happiest moment of his life… the sudden, good, safe feeling of father and mother and little brother; of a place where he belonged, where he loved and was loved. And by his equals.'

Perhaps this hints at why Edith stayed with Hubert and adopted his illegitimate children – she believed the strength and security of the family is paramount. And the loss of her own father as a child is remembered in the lines:

> 'They say there is no other
> Can take the place of mother.
> I say there is no one I'd rather
> See than my father.'

Edith had always been determined to support herself and not rely on the state, expecting everyone else to do the same for a happy, functional society:

> 'For anything we want very much, on our own exertions and work
> and not to expect to glide easily into the haven where we would
> be towed at the apron strings on an angel goddess.'

But now she was in her fifties, Edith's hedonistic lifestyle was catching up with her, both financially and physically, as her famous stores of energy were gradually losing reserves. Her poor business management skills and careless treatment of money meant that she and Hubert had not made provision for the winter of their lives and the prospect of senior age was looking somewhat bleak. She wrote to Harry:

> 'We live very quietly now that the girls are married and Hubert's
> eyes are so bad. Any success my stories have had is due I think
> to a sort of light-hearted outlook on life – and now that Hubert's
> eyes have failed him a steam-roller seems to have gone over all
> one's hopes and ambitions, and it is difficult to remember how it
> felt to be light-hearted.'

Most troubling of all was that the children were increasingly distancing themselves from their mother, the beloved children's author E. Nesbit, who had devoted a lifetime thinking about and writing for young people, at the expense of her own family.

Chapter 17

A Tragic Farewell

'…he has left his impress, not only upon all those who knew him but upon hundreds of thousands who never saw his face and hardly knew his name. His ideas have contributed to the intellectual make-up of innumerable men and women…'

Cecil Chesterton on Hubert Bland

Tuesday was deadline day for Hubert, and on 14 April 1914 he sat in his study dictating to Alice a review for the *New Statesman* of two novels that she had read to him a few days before. Satisfied with the story, Hubert stood up but was immediately overcome with an alarming dizziness. 'Mouse, I feel giddy,' he cried. Alice sensed something was wrong and ran from her desk to the door to call for help. As she rushed back to try to hold Hubert up, he slowly sank to his knees on the hearthrug. It was here in front of the fire that he spoke his final words, 'It's all right – I'm not hurt.' Hubert died there with Alice and she held him in her arms until the doctor arrived and confirmed he had suffered an enormous heart attack.

Edith had been forced to share her husband throughout his life and so it was to be at his death, for she was some eighty miles away at their Sussex cottage, Crowlink, unaware of the dramatic events at Well Hall. Ironically, she was finishing her novel *The Incredible Honeymoon*, writing about a young couple's happy future just as her own thirty-four-year marriage came to an end. Alice sent her an urgent telegram: 'Come at once Hubert very ill'. Immediately ordering a taxi from Eastbourne, Edith sat in silence for the interminable journey. It was 2am when she finally arrived home where she dashed at once to Hubert's side as he lay lifeless on the sofa. Refusing to believe he had gone she desperately tried to warm her husband's body with hot water bottles and a quilt – just as she had done with her beloved Fabian whose death still haunted her thirteen years later. It was only when the doctor opened one of Hubert's veins that Edith finally accepted the truth, and broke down. She felt as if her life had 'broken off short' by his death. 'It was a time of horrible misery,' said Alice Hoatson afterwards. Edith had a death mask made of Hubert's face, carefully wrapping it in silk and placing it on the mantelpiece.

Hubert's funeral was held four days later on 18 April and he was buried at Woolwich Cemetery next to his parents. Reverend Francis Jeffrey held the service, a Catholic one in respect of Hubert's conversion some thirteen years before, and it is estimated about forty people paid their respects. For a man who had a million readers of his *Sunday Chronicle* column, it seems a small funeral. But even stranger is the obituary that appeared in that newspaper and also the *New Statesman*. Neither mentioned Edith, and what was worse, the *Sunday Chronicle* ran two paragraphs about Alice. Edith was shocked, furious and deeply hurt by the deliberate oversight. Alice called it 'the most insulting and impossible laudation – meant as praise, no doubt, but dreadful to me, and to Edith too.' The final blow was when Edith realised Hubert had snubbed her in his will; he left the balance of his estate (£900) in trust to his favourite son John, with Edith to receive only the household goods and not a penny more. He wrote, '...my wife is happily able to earn a good income and my other children are provided for'. Edith almost went mad with grief over it all. Hubert died just a week before their thirty-fourth wedding anniversary. It had been a marriage that had endured bankruptcy, two bouts of smallpox, stillbirth, two miscarriages, the death of a son, multiple affairs on both sides and the adoption of two illegitimate children. Perhaps in death, Hubert handed his wife the ultimate insult for a marriage in which he felt unappreciated; in one of his famous columns for the *Sunday Chronicle*, he wrote about how much easier his life would have been if he had been born female. Compiled in 1898 and called 'If I Were a Woman', there is no doubt that it was written humorously but perhaps there is a grain of truth behind the jokes?

> '...the writer "Hubert" has had a hard time of it on the whole. He has toiled long and caught nothing to speak of; he has acquired many more kicks than halfpence. It is true he has warmed both hands at the fire of life [is this code for his affairs?], but he has burnt his fingers badly more than once. He is an unappreciated, a misunderstood man, and he has been forced reluctantly to the conclusion that the world is not a good place for good men.'

Edith was inconsolable after Hubert's death and she attempted to cope with her unbearable loss by finding solace in writing, just as she had done after Fabian died. She edited and published a collection of Hubert's columns from the *Sunday Chronicle*, called *Essays by Hubert* and published them during the year of his passing in 1914. In the epilogue she wrote of him tenderly:

'Hubert wrote as he spoke and he spoke as he thought. He never did for money or for fame sell himself. He had in the highest degree, the quality of intellectual honesty. He would not deceive himself, nor would he suffer others to be deceived. His was the large tolerance of one who understands the weakness and the strength of the soul of man. He hated the Pharisees, the Prigs, the Puritans. All men else he loved. Two years before his death blindness came upon him, blindness for which there was no hope of cure, blindness darkening the world daily more and more. Hubert met it like a man… Hubert worked to the last, he died working, and his last words when he felt the hand of death upon him were "I am not hurt".'

Hubert's great follower Cecil Chesterton wrote the introduction to *Essays by Hubert* and praised him for being a respected journalist throughout his 'exciting controversial career', describing his columns as 'almost a high-water mark of English journalism'. Just as tabloid journalists do today, Hubert's great skill was to explain complicated news stories in simple language and encourage the masses to become interested in the issues of the day. Chesterton concluded:

'Bland always took the view that normal men take, although he argued the case for that view more ably than ordinary men can argue … he has left his impress, not only upon all those who knew him but upon hundreds of thousands who never saw his face and hardly knew his name. His ideas have contributed to the intellectual make-up of innumerable men and women who have diverged in various ways from the faith which he held… [he] expressed by himself with an energy, a lucidity, and a picturesqueness which we shall not easily see again.'

Although his columns seem somewhat pompous and outdated today, Hubert dedicated thirty years to writing about socialism and spent his spare time volunteering with the Fabian Society as honorary treasurer, lecturer and active member. He wasn't a moral man; through his clothes and speech he built up a false persona of a learned gentleman, and his incurable philandering deeply hurt his wife and his family as well as other women. He was a vain poseur. But it can't be denied that his commitment to socialism throughout his life helped to change the political landscape of Britain forever.

Later that year to ease her grief, Edith went to Paris with John to rest and recuperate. She stayed for four months before suffering severe stomach

125

pains and wrote to Well Hall to ask for help to return home. Alice Hoatson volunteered and brought Edith back to Eltham in mid-May. When Edith's illness continued, the doctor diagnosed her with a stomach ulcer and sent her to Guy's Hospital for an operation. In those days, the procedure was considered serious and the following day Edith almost died after her temperature dropped dangerously low. When Iris came to visit her mother, the surgeon explained that it was unlikely she would survive. But Edith refused to give up and insisted that all she needed was something to eat. Although the doctor strongly advised 'nil by mouth', Iris made the life-changing decision to take the matter into her own hands and rushed out to buy nourishment. Every hour of that day Iris gently and carefully fed her mother half a teaspoonful of Brand's essence of beef. By the end of the day a miracle happened. Edith's temperature rose and she was out of the danger zone; she would live. Beating all the odds, Edith's health gradually improved and by September she was able to return home. Her brush with death hit her hard, both mentally and physically. Six weeks after being discharged, she was still in horrendous pain and when examined, it was discovered the ulcer hadn't healed properly. Edith remained desperately weak and sank into deep depression as two women nursed her through it – her friend Elsa Courlander and Alice. How would Edith have felt being cared for by the woman who for most of her marriage had come between her and Hubert? Perhaps she was just glad to be alive. Three months later, she wrote, 'Even now [I] am only able to get up to crawl about the house for part of the day.' Alice recalls that time in her memoir, writing that Edith was so grateful to the doctors and nurses at Guy's Hospital for saving her life that she gave a cheque for £7 to thank the matron. 'She was quite the naughtiest patient they ever had but they all loved her and she was the life and soul of the ward'. Another witness remembers Edith's determination to get well after her illness and the loss of Hubert, '…depression in the autumn of that year hung heavy over Well Hall, yet her irrepressible hilarity shone through the clouds'.

This illness was the second time Edith thought she had come close to death. Some years earlier, she had been diagnosed with cancer of the stomach and given a 1 in 100 chance of survival. In true Edith style, she held a party to say goodbye to her friends. 'Whatever her own apprehensions were in the matter, she carried us through the evening with colours flying, apparently in the happiest spirits possible. And of course we all played up to her example to the best of our ability,' said party-guest Laurence Housman, the actor. In fact, the celebrations turned out to be unnecessary because when Edith was examined by a specialist he said she was perfectly healthy, aside from her bronchitis and asthma – the only health issues she would have even as an old person. Housman said, 'The next time I saw my hostess, all was well over.

Then she said to me, "Well, anyway, I found out I wasn't afraid of death!" And the discovery gave her great satisfaction.'

But although Edith recovered, after Hubert's death things were never the same again at Well Hall. The divide between the children worsened when Edith gave various of his personal possessions to them all except for Rosamund, who accused her adoptive mother of 'a very distinct streak of cruelty'. It was at this time that John discovered the truth of his birth when he was rude to Alice and the secret that she was his mother was at last revealed. Hubert's death had finally unlocked a fateful concealment that had been hidden for so long, and Alice and Edith were left facing each other – alone at last after a lifetime of one person binding them together. They had lived under the same roof for all their adult lives, a feat that would have been impressive enough for anyone but, considering the circumstances, it was extraordinary. Edith felt bitterness and a sense of betrayal after all that her friend had put her through. The diminutive and competent Alice, who had remained loyal to the family as the mousy housekeeper, was now left with nothing – not even the respect of her own children. Her big brown eyes and mop of grey hair seemed to shrink ever further into the background as she watched the family broken, divided and grieving. Yet something far worse was to come: it was the eve of the First World War. Edith had always written about long-lost fathers; now Great Britain was about to lose a generation of sons in the most terrible circumstances.

Chapter 18

The War

'The Fields of Flanders' E. Nesbit (1915)

'And the flower of hopes, and flowers of dreams,
The noble, fruitful, beautiful schemes,
The tree of life with its fruit and bud,
Are trampled down in the mud and the blood.'

There was an eerie throbbing above Well Hall and, a few moments later, the chilling sound of an explosion. Everyone rushed outside. 'We saw the Zeppelins and heard the firing and saw the rockets and the searchlights,' Edith would later write of the bomb that demolished a new house in Well Hall Road in August 1916. Had the pilot aimed just a fraction differently, Edith would have been killed and Well Hall razed to the ground; the mansion continued to be at risk when an unexploded bomb was discovered in the garden later in the war. As the sirens wailed their awful moan, signalling yet another air raid, Edith prayed the fighting would be over before her youngest, John, 15, would be sent away. She always made coffee for the tram drivers who were forced to stop driving during air raids, and it was when she was handing out mugs on the top of a tram that she saw her most horrific image of war when a German zeppelin was shot down in flames. She wept as she watched the burning, blackened human bodies fall from the sky.

On 28 June 1914 the assassination of Franz Ferdinand, archduke of Austria-Hungary, triggered the beginning of the First World War. Although no one could know the full extent of the horrific events that were about to unfold, people in Britain were sensible of the frightening implications of a global conflict. The backdrop of international events was felt keenly by Edith, who was at one of the lowest points of her life. Almost entirely alone in her enormous empty house, she was shattered by the loss of her husband, weak from her recent illness and poor after medical expenses and her bad management of money. She had developed bronchitis and constantly battled to give up smoking. Her confidence was low – without Hubert she had become nervous of strangers and was sensitive about how people saw her. Her work for the *Strand Magazine* and other periodicals had all but dried up. All she had left were memories of a home that had once seen such life and jubilation – the wild Bohemian parties; the celebrations of her literary work; the friends that had been rejoiced over. Edith's illness had aged her, and Well Hall was a visual representation of her family's faded grandeur. The once magnificent garden had grown wild, the inside of the house slowly shabbier. Although Ada Breakell had been living for some years next to Well Hall in one of the cottages on the grounds known as North Lodge, most of Edith's friends were occupied with the war effort elsewhere, leaving her almost deserted and reduced to doing her own housekeeping. Some of her male friends such as her former lover Gerald Gould would never return from the fighting. As for her children, Iris was working at Woolwich Arsenal in charge of munitions workers. Rosamund was with her husband in Sweden as he served on a secret government mission in the Baltics. Paul signed up as a sapper with the London Electrical Engineers and was stationed in Newhaven. The youngest, 15-year-old John, was training with the OTC as a student at the City of London School. A single ray of hope in Edith's life was her only grandchild, Pandora, now six years old. The little girl had come to live at Well Hall and Edith doted on her. With her long hair, bright eyes and adorable smile, many commented on Pandora's likeness to her grandmother and the two were close. Unfortunately, the girl was without a father as Iris' marriage to Austin Philips hadn't been a happy one. Iris had been forced to become an independent woman (with shades of Edith's resilience as a young mother), setting herself up as a dressmaker before the war at Edith's flat in London, which had moved from Royalty Chambers to Rathbone Place, off Tottenham Court Road. Iris shared the rent with her mother before moving back to Well Hall with Pandora to work at the munitions factory when war broke out.

Of course, there was one other person who remained with Edith. The Mouse continued to live at Well Hall and took it upon herself to organise the money side of things, an area of housekeeping that Edith hated and was hopeless at. Edith had spent every penny as she earned it – and more – entertaining, renting her various homes and helping others, and by now she was in quite considerable financial difficulty. Nearing retirement age in 1915, she wrote to the Society of Authors asking if they thought she had any chance of getting assistance from the government:

> 'I wish I could get a pension! … If I had a certain income, however small, I could contentedly spend what's left of my life in making do. And I can't write. The spring seems broken.'

Eventually it was Maurice Hewlett, a well-known historical novelist of the time, who secured a civil pension for Edith, of £60 a year for her services to literature (for her poetry rather than her children's novels). Although the money didn't stretch far (and Edith greatly begrudged the income tax), at least it provided some much-needed support. Rudyard Kipling helped her get a small pension from the Society of Authors, although their friendship had soured after Edith held a grudge against him for 'plagiarising' *The Story of the Amulet*, which she claimed gave him the idea for the time-travelling plot for *Puck of Pook's Hill* (1906). In fact, both books were published about the same time so it is unlikely Kipling copied from her.

This wasn't the first time Edith had hit rock bottom, it had happened more than a decade earlier with the death of her son Fabian in 1900. Then her grief had triggered a period of prolific writing, when she published her most famous novels in quick succession. But this time, the words would not come. Instead, she channelled her sorrow into a frenzied (and somewhat fruitless) obsession with an obscure theory that it was Sir Frances Bacon who wrote Shakespeare's plays. For years, it took up an enormous amount of her time and money and she went almost mad over it. Her extraordinary memory meant she could recite passages from Shakespeare yet in her letters to friends she wrote of her great sadness in possessing not a single shred of impetus for commercial work:

> 'I wish I could write some more about Roberta and Phyllis and Peter but I feel sometimes as though I should never write anything again – worth reading or writing, that is.'

Edith's daughter Iris remembers how distressed her mother was at the time:

> '...she really wrote very little after my father's death. He used to encourage her and she missed his appreciation. She was really rather knocked out by his death... The kinds of children's stories she was best at were dragged out of her after that time by necessity alone and not any real desire to write although she buried her distress by going deeper and deeper into the Bacon Shakespeare curiosity.'

As the atrocities of the Great War destroyed the innocence of Great Britain, Edith found the horrors of the fighting difficult to comprehend and was constantly anxious that Paul would be sent abroad from Newhaven with the

London Electrical Engineers. But she did as she had done many times before and remained resilient. Edith had her roots on the land, having been born on the grounds of her father's agricultural college. She always preferred the countryside to the city and as a young woman she was inspired by the Arts and Crafts Movement's belief in a simpler, nobler way of life. Perhaps it was her deep connection with the land which inspired Edith to move on to the next chapter of her life and transform Well Hall into a market garden and a boarding house for paying guests (PGs or pigs as she nicknamed them). Many of the boarders worked at the large munitions factory in Woolwich some three miles away, and some stayed a few weeks, others for months. Although Edith had always offered an open house to friends, having complete strangers was entirely different – especially as some guests didn't take very good care of her lovely home. But having people around her again gave Edith a focus and she worked hard to provide them with a comfortable place to stay. In her late fifties by this time, Edith had minimal paid help as most of the domestic staff had left or had to be let go. Yet despite all the hard work, she eked out moments of joy; as a friend once wrote of her, 'More than anyone I've ever met she could create out of ordinary day-by-day affairs, incidents of fun, of romance, of beauty, of poetry.' She relished eating outside, for example. And she still maintained her sense of absurdity when one of the cook's sons, 11-year-old Pelham, fell into a large pot of marmalade one day. From then on, whenever the marmalade was passed around at breakfast, everyone jokingly asked for some Pelham. Later, a war wedding cheered everyone up when the cook's sister, Adelaide, married her sweetheart Harry and celebrated at Well Hall. 'I enjoyed it – & I don't enjoy many things now,' wrote Edith.

Characteristically, no matter how low her mood or how hard she'd worked on the land that day, Edith couldn't resist rallying herself up – and others – with her home-grown entertainments. In her famous bohemian way, the company was eclectic, from Mrs Evans who ran the poultry farm to random munitions workers and the local sanitary inspector mixed with Edith's literary set such as Lady Roderick Jones who arrived by motorbike. Edith loved organising fancy dress dances for the children of her paying guests and made outfits for them out of whatever she could find, spending ages making sure everything was just perfect. She enjoyed her new little friends and her knack for putting children at ease hadn't left her; she would invite them up into her room to sit with her to listen to stories or help her make a dress or mend a sheet. Once dinner was over, there was a ritual of washing teacups in a wooden bowl in the dining room, and it was a privilege for one of the children to be asked to join in. One little girl who lived with Edith during the war was Joan Evans Alonso whose mother helped with the poultry farm. Joan stayed at Well Hall from 1915 until 1921:

> 'People, laughter, games, fun, good conversation – there was plenty of all these… the order of the day – of our daily life – was shadowed, prodded, and shared by E. Nesbit's warm, enveloping personality… E. Nesbit's greatest gift to us children was that she, this very talented and busy woman, was generous – generous with herself, her time, her pleasures, her friends, her flowers, her fun. She seemed to have time for us all, to need us, to enjoy us.'

Many of Edith's old Fabian friends, playwrights and young poets still came to visit including Cecil Chesterton, Bernard Shaw and H.G. Wells. But as the war continued and the old Fabian group grew apart, Shaw and Wells visited less and less. In the evenings, the large drawing room was used for charades and dancing when Rosamund and Pandora led waltzes to old-fashioned lilting music; Edith or Ada would accompany them on the piano. These evenings were frequently interrupted by the wail of the air-raid siren, when everyone would assemble in the stone-floored dining room and Edith would hand out coffee while they waited.

Like the rest of the country, Well Hall was on rations. Each paying guest had their own coloured jar with a measure of sugar and butter or margarine, and on a Thursday, everyone could swap their rations if they wanted, apparently resulting in fierce bargaining. Some of the rations would be shared for communal cooking and there wasn't a scrap of food wasted. Edith had to use every housekeeping trick she knew, including a rather unusual method of cooking using a hay-box cooker, a large insulated box with two round, deep holes. Food would first be boiled in casserole dishes and then put into the cooker between hot iron discs. The lid was sealed and the casseroles would be left to tenderise. Using produce from the garden, Edith also enjoyed making jam, 'We've settled not to have any lunch as its war time!' she once joked to a visitor, handing them a spoon. To supplement the rations, Edith rolled up her sleeves, picked up her spade and dug for victory – albeit doing so in her own indomitable style with silver bangles jangling and cigarettes dangling. Partly to save herself, partly for the war effort, it was in the summer of 1915 that her sale of garden produce began in earnest. The old orchard was turned into allotments and she (and others) grew cabbages and other vegetables and fruit for the government as well as flowers for military hospitals. She began a chicken farm when her customers started asking for eggs. An early adopter of battery-hen practices, she would shine a light on her chickens to make them lay faster with the result that in one week her hens produced 1,100 eggs. There was a joke that Well Hall was a munitions factory because it filled shells (the egg variety). The green badminton lawn became dotted with poultry coops, prize-bred ducks swam in the moat and hens pottered about by the banks. It was hard work, and Edith would stand up all day on Fridays and Saturdays making up big bunches of sweet old-fashioned flowers to sell to men who worked nearby building the garden suburb and the munitions huts. They would buy a bunch or two for their wives or mothers on their way home. 'It's a queer life, but I think it's the best that could befall me just now,' Edith remarked. In February 1915, she wrote to Harry:

> 'I am much better in health – but I do not find I can take much interest in life. Without Hubert everything is so unmeaning. I don't do much writing, though I am always hoping I shall be able to again. I have taken in paying guests since October – If I could get a few more I should get on all right. Also I sell flowers out of the garden, and apples and vegetables. In the last eight weeks I have made by that alone 25/–a week. Then there is the pension. If I could live without writing I should like never to write another line. The war makes everything more miserable. It seems too horrible to be true.'

One of the most upsetting moments of the war was when a German bomb intended for the East India Docks killed eighteen schoolchildren; Well Hall lay just five miles from the East End of London, and Edith was greatly saddened by those events of 13 June 1917. Living so close to the train station, when the hospital locomotives pulled in Edith and her band of helpers would go down to visit and entertain the wounded. Yet her sense of humanity was tempered by her violent patriotism, which lost her friends including E.M. Forster. She compiled an anthology of war poems, *Battle Songs* (1914), and wrote an article attacking the Germans. 'I felt it my duty… It was a horrible thing to do, but I did it,' she wrote to Harry. Later, in November 1917, the *Daily Mail* published *The Haunted Garden*, Edith's tribute to the soldiers who died in the war.

Edward Andrade was serving in France as an officer in the Royal Garrison Artillery. Later he became a captain, and Edith wrote regularly to her 'dearest Edward Edward', sharing her news of home:

> '…with this war going on the world seems so unreal that doing any writing seems futile. It feels like beginning an epic on the morning of the Last Day, with the last trumps sounding in your ears…'

Finally, Edith wrote:

> 'Everything seems pretty average hell just now… I have written
> one or two articles & poems – but I don't seem to have the heart
> for writing. Nothing seems worthwhile somehow. It is like doing
> work on the sea shore when you know the tide is soon coming in
> that will wash away you & your work altogether….'

But she kept her head above water and steadily continued swimming. Refusing
to give up on life, she slowly regained her mental and physical strength as she
transformed her stately home into a working co-operative farm. Remarkably,
Edith herself was about to be transformed as she emerged from mourning the
loss of Hubert to finding safety and security with a very dear companion.

Chapter 19

Her Final Romantic Hero

'For the first time in my life, I know what it is to possess a man's whole heart.'

Edith in a letter to her friend Berta Ruck

In the summer of 1916, Edith unexpectedly fell in love again. It was at one of the garden party fetes held in the grounds of Well Hall to raise money for the local Labour Party. Thomas Terry Tucker, nicknamed the Skipper, was a captain of the Woolwich Ferry paddle steamer that chugged across the Thames. Described as a jolly cockney sparrow by those who knew him, he was the absolute antithesis of Hubert – chubby, cheerful and tiny. Born a twin in Bermondsey, Skipper had eight brothers and sisters. He began as a rivet boy on torpedo boats and worked his way up the nautical ladder, being awarded Freedom of the River and sailing across the world including to New York.

The only thing Skipper had in common with Hubert was their shared enthusiasm for socialism, which was how they met. Skipper had been friends with Edith and Hubert for some thirty-five years, since they met during the early days of the Fabian Society, probably at a lecture by George Bernard Shaw in Essex Hall in the Strand. Skipper organised Sunday afternoon meetings at Poplar Town Hall, where Shaw and friends of Edith and Hubert frequently spoke. Skipper volunteered on the board of three local schools and was selected in 1909 and 1912 by the Labour Party as a candidate for the River Ward in the Woolwich Borough Council elections, although he was unsuccessful both times. Skipper and his wife Sophia, an attractive local machinist known for her community work, met Edith and Hubert again through their shared interests in the Labour Party in the Well Hall area of Eltham. Before the war, Skipper would sometimes go to Well Hall with his wife to talk politics with Hubert, who enjoyed their conversations. After Hubert went blind, Skipper would visit him regularly to bring him local socialist news.

Edith and Sophia were both part of the Women's Pioneer Campaign Committee, which was connected with the Woolwich Labour Party; women weren't allowed to join the Labour Party proper. Sophia was famous for organising fundraising bazaars as well as teas and socials and Edith began opening the grounds of Well Hall every summer for a fundraising garden party. The community relished the chance to peep inside the mysterious and grand old manor house, a famous local landmark that few had been into. The garden was brought alive with hundreds of people paying sixpence a ticket to enjoy the old English country garden, with ices on the lawn, a baby show, a palm reader and boating on the moat in the *Lucky Duck*, captained by Paul and launched by the Skipper who famously lost the champagne for its maiden voyage. Skipper was an enthusiastic helper, one year selling 100 tickets and making a cake that was sold to the highest bidder. 'We are officially informed that there have been no casualties as a result of the consumption of the cakes,' it was recorded in the local press. Edith sold signed copies of her books and gave piano solos, and there were sports races for children and adults; one year, Edith's granddaughter Pandora won the girls aged eight to ten years running event. At the end of the party, Edith was thanked in great ceremony but she gracefully declined any gratitude and always insisted it was the Skipper who had done all the hard work.

In January 1916, Sophia died after a long period of poor health; she had been virtually an invalid for years. She was laid to rest not 100 yards from where Fabian was buried at the local parish church in Eltham, and Edith sent a wreath to remember Sophia by. It was after his wife's death that Skipper noticed that his old friend Edith was struggling. He wrote later:

> 'I saw her getting more and more weary from work and worry. My first wife had died and I went often because I could make myself useful. She seemed so lonely and I often found her crying and in low spirits.'

He would go around to Well Hall to offer practical help with the house and gardening, such as moving the little wooden hut in the garden where Edith sold her fruit, vegetables and flowers. He thought she would sell more if it was on the front lawn facing Well Hall Road. He added a seat and a gas fire to make it more comfortable for both Edith and Alice, for she helped sell the produce too. Edith happily described her first day working with Skipper in a letter to Paul who was still serving in the war as an engineer in Newhaven:

> 'We opened the hut-shop today, taking nearly £5 for eggs and vegetables and flowers. I am sure we shall be able to sell everything we can rake together out of the garden. We got a drainpipe and set a jug of lilac and flags on top so that it showed from the road, and

had a hen coop with 3 hens and a cock to attract customers! We are very comfortable now, with Louise (the cook) and a woman who comes in. I do not have to do so much house-work. We make our own bread: it is a fair treat, after the baker's stuff which is making everybody ill… I was on my feet today from 8.30 to 8.15 so I am pretty tired: but I am very well. And Mr Tucker keeps up my spirits and prevents my worrying over trifles.'

After gently gaining her trust, Skipper helped organise Edith's finances, which were in a complete mess. Next, he dealt with the other difficulties in her life, such as awkward paying guests. Some of the people staying at Well Hall had become a nuisance, which worried Edith greatly. She was so generous and hospitable that she couldn't bear to ask anyone to leave but some, such as a man called Russell Green, took terrible advantage of her by staying at weekends and regularly bringing various family members uninvited. After asking nicely without success, Skipper swore at him in the garden and got rid of him.

Just a few years apart in age, the two lonely fifty-somethings began to grow close. Edith had never been self-conscious about getting older as she once said, 'I have had six years of youth longer than most women, and I have enjoyed every moment of them.' They say that opposites attract and Skipper's easy-going personality and practical capabilities were a foil for the highly-strung Edith. He may not have had a formal cultural education, yet he was solid, wise and had travelled the world as a marine engineer. He put up with Edith's fastidiousness and petulance with good humour and made the grand dame laugh after her years of unhappiness. Both were energetic and unafraid of hard work, had known the other's spouse and found comfort in talking about their lost partners. During his gradual courtship, Edith became physically attracted to Skipper. Years of being independent, resilient and generous had left her worn out and poor and although she wasn't looking for a knight in shining armour, she let herself be girlishly swept up in Skipper's arms as he tenderly saved her in the most romantic way. She said simply, 'I like to be near him.' Edith described their relationship to Harry:

'After the cold misery of the last three years I feel as though someone had come and put a fur cloak round me. Or like one shipwrecked on a lonely island, and I have found another shipwrecked mariner to help me to build a hut and make a fire.'

Edith took Paul into her confidence about her new love affair and they talked late into the night about whether Skipper would make a good husband for her.

Typically humble, Skipper described how they got engaged after he came across Edith in tears at Well Hall:

> 'One day I said: "It looks to me as if you want a tug around here."
> She said she wished she had one. So she married me very soon after.'

At the risk of spoiling his story, Edith in fact refused Skipper's first proposal but was persuaded to change her mind, as she delightedly explained to Harry:

> 'I have had a horrible three years since Hubert died, shivering in a sort of Arctic night, and about six months ago I had an offer of marriage from a marine engineer, the best man I have ever known. I said "No", and he then said he was very sorry I could not care for him, but that would not prevent his devoting the rest of his life to me and if ever I needed a friend's help he would be there. He has been very, very kind and helpful ever since Hubert died, and after I refused him he quietly devoted himself to my interests in every way – helping with the poultry farm, finding men to work for me – and so on. Presently I found he had refused an appointment with £100 rise in salary. I asked him why and he told me that it was because he would not leave the neighbourhood where I was. So then I began to think it was rather a one-sided arrangement, and that perhaps life would be less wretched if one could make hands with a good friend and chum who believed that one could make him happy. And after a good deal of hesitation I talked it over with my son Paul, and at last said Yes.'

Skipper made an honest woman of Edith on 20 February 1917 at St Peter the Apostle Church, Woolwich. A Catholic place of worship, St Peter's must have been chosen by Edith as Skipper was stoutly Church of England. Ironically, it lies about a mile away from where Hubert was born. Exactly a century to the day after the wedding took place, St Peter's stands proudly in the midst of a busy community. It remains a grand building, designed by Augustus Pugin who was one of the architects of the Houses of Parliament in Westminster. Its striking turquoise blue ceiling shines like a blue sky of optimism, making it a very different wedding from when a heavily pregnant Edith hastily married Hubert in a registry office some thirty-six years before. Both weddings shared something unfortunate however; the lack of a wedding breakfast. Illness forced Edith and Skipper to cancel their reception – February 1917 was infamously cold and several of the guests were quite ill, including Alice Hoatson with neuritis and Edith's son-in-law Clifford, who had congestion on his lungs. A week before the wedding Edith wrote, 'In these dismal circumstances I can't have a party.' As the life and soul of social gatherings, Edith must have been disappointed not to have celebrated her nuptials. But nothing could dampen her radiant delight in becoming Mrs Bland-Tucker, as she now referred to herself. 'I was married last Tuesday. I am very happy,' Edith wrote to Harry, sending him a photo of her new husband:

> 'He is the soul of goodness and kindness, and he never blunders in matters of sentiment or emotion. He doesn't blunder in anything, for the matter of that, but you know in those matters how fatally easy it is to go wrong … his whole life seems to have been spent in doing good. Also he is fond of laughter, and likes the same kind of jokes that please me. I am very, very happy. I feel as though I had opened another volume of the book of life (the last volume) and it is full of beautiful stories and poetry.'

Edith's new husband mellowed her and Edith responded to his love and care by becoming more mature and less offended by others. 'I used to tell Edith to say to hell with a lot of things that troubled her. She got quite adept and was the better for it,' wrote the Skipper about his wife. One of Edith's friends remarked that her personality changed markedly after her marriage, 'Those who didn't know her during her last five years (after she married Mr Tucker) can never realise how much simpler and how much more tolerant she became.' Edith had always been easily influenced by those she loved and she subconsciously adopted the Skipper's uncomplicated ways: 'She had not a streak of malice in her,' he said of his wife. They began calling each other the pet name 'Mate', and the Skipper's love for Edith seemed to melt away her resentment, and in none of his recollections of his wife does Skipper mention her famous temper tantrums:

> 'Let me tell you that the greatest quality in her character was the quality of forgiveness. She couldn't hold the slightest ill feeling against anyone, no matter what they did to her. I never knew a living creature with less venom. And when I came to her, I was 60 years of age, and had had a fair experience of the world.'

After the wedding, Edith went to stay with Skipper at his small house, refurnishing it and referring to it as the Refuge. Superstitious, Edith would kneel and pray when she went into Sophia's room in the hope that Skipper's first wife would look kindly on her and their marriage. Edith tenderly describes being there together:

> 'We sat on a sofa with my head on his shoulder, and fell happily asleep, both of us. This means lots as you know. It is extraordinarily rum that I should have found someone who suits me like this. It is like a consolation prize for all sorts of failures. And the knowledge that I have a friend and comrade to sit on the other side of the hearth where life's dying embers fade is incredibly comforting.'

Shortly after, the newlyweds moved in to Well Hall together and Edith's children reacted to their new stepfather in different ways. Paul was married two months after his mother, on 23 April. His wife, Gertrude Nebel, of German parents, was rather prim about becoming connected to Skipper's working-class background, which made Paul unhappy. Edith tried hard to befriend Gertrude, a primary school teacher from Deptford – the same place Edith had hosted her Christmas parties for underprivileged children all those years ago. But Edith found her a rather prickly character and didn't think her good enough for her son. In truth, the poor girl was in awe of Edith when she met her and for some time afterwards, because of her mother-in-law's literary success and grand manner. She called Edith Mrs Bland, which Edith hated as it reminded her of Hubert's mother, who she hadn't got on with. Eventually, Edith wrote a funny verse to encourage her new daughter-in-law to call her by a different name and they decided on MIL and DIL (short for mother-in-law and daughter-in-law). The first verse goes:

> 'Gertrude, holding Paul's dear hand,
> Do not call me "Mrs Bland".
> Call me "Jane" or "Bet" or "Sue",
> Anything but what you do!'

The newlyweds lived at Well Hall, which was large enough for the next generation to stay and Edith made an effort to be friends with her, dedicating a collection of poetry to serious Gertrude. In a way, Edith's marriage to the Skipper helped to heal her fractious relationship with her children. The war had brought them all back to Well Hall and the new, mellow Edith began to love them anew. Iris, after her own unhappy marriage, didn't understand her mother wanting to marry again. But Rosamund liked Skipper and became the closest to him of all of Edith's children. 'You're the only one who has been kind to me about this,' wept Edith to her daughter, who asked her, 'He's not Tommy Tucker, I hope?'. Edith laughed as she cried and replied, 'That's the worst of it. He is!' Years later, after Edith died, Rosamund went to live with Skipper to help him through the grief.

It's not known how John felt about Skipper, although Edith's quote to Rosamund suggests he wasn't supportive. Perhaps as a student still at school he might have felt confused at the prospect of a stepfather and one who was so different from Hubert. It was a sentiment few could stop themselves from commenting on, including Edith herself. 'Everyone is much surprised at my marrying Mr Tucker – but no one more surprised than I am,' she wrote, explaining why she chose such a different second husband:

> 'The fact that he isn't literary makes everything possible. I couldn't have married anyone who came anywhere near to competing with Hubert. But this man is different: his only points of resemblance… are his sane Socialist view of life, his sense of humour, and his love for me. I feel fur-wrapped from the cold of old age. Wrapped, indeed, in furs of price, for he is (as my gardener said of him) an "only" man. There is no one like him. I grow fonder of him every day.'

Although both of Edith's husbands were born into the working class, it reveals a great deal of their personalities that Skipper embraced this while Hubert fought his whole life against it. Hubert prided himself on his outward appearance of the gentleman, complete with monocle and velvet jacket but Skipper wore his straggly beard long (it waggled when he chattered) and never wore a collar at home. Skipper dropped his 'h' while Hubert was conscious about the way he spoke. A deeper divide between them was their morality. Skipper was committed to the Church of England and thought it unforgivable that a woman should belong to anyone but her husband. We will never know whether he knew the colourful details of Edith's bohemian past – but it doesn't seem to matter. For Skipper, Edith was a majestic woman. For Edith, she was both amazed and comforted that she had found someone so devoted to her in both a romantic and practical way. 'For the first time in my life, I know what it is to possess a man's whole heart,' she wrote to her friend, Berta Ruck.

As the First World War finally ended, Edith had another reason to celebrate when Paul was brought home from Newhaven with the London Electrical

Engineers. She wrote on 11 November 1918, 'Thank God for this day! Now our boy is safe!' With the fighting over and a solid friend by her side, Edith wrote to Harry about how safe she felt with her new husband:

> 'I feel peaceful and contented in my new life with him. He is the best man I have ever known, and he has a philosophy of life which makes all things easy to him. He never worries and he never lets me worry – so, though we are pinched for money, and hard put to it to keep going I am quite at ease. He cares absolutely nothing for material things and possessions, though he enjoys life and is very merry and jolly. He has been all over the world as ship's engineer and is a born observer. Also he has words to clothe his thoughts and observations. If we had time I am sure we could do some good writing work together. I send you a paper with a sketch in it I wrote with Mr Tucker's help, and an article about a ship.'

Edith settled into her second marriage by acting the role of a domestic wife, not one that she had ever played with Hubert. She delighted in bringing little presents home for her Skipper, such as a special cigar if she had gone up into London to meet her publisher. She would wait up for him until the early hours of the morning to come home from running the Woolwich ferry, keeping his dinner for him and they would stay up chatting until sunrise. Other times, she would go to work with him, cook a beefsteak and make him coffee in the cabin of the boat. He called her Cook, which she adored. On Sunday evenings in the long drawing room at Well Hall, she played the piano while he would dance the hornpipe or they'd play cards together. The couple wrote up old sea shanty tales and sold them to magazines such as the *Westminster Gazette*. One of the Skipper's true stories is 'Tammy Lee's Jack', which was published in *Five of Us – and Madeline*, edited by Rosamund in 1925. Edith continued to freelance for magazines such as *New Witness* and the *New Statesman* but there would be no more children's books. She sadly remarked once that it was because publishers didn't care for her children's novels as her stories had fallen out of fashion. 'Publishers tell me that children don't want my sort of books any more,' she wrote. Her pension is estimated to have been not more than £60 a year, less than £3,000 in today's money. Royalties from her work would have also been coming in and she sold her letters from H.G. Wells and Rudyard Kipling for cash but even with her income from the farm and paying guests, it all added up to far less than required to keep Well Hall going – heating bills alone were more than £4,000 a year. Carpets became threadbare, the bath sagged and the gardens became rambling.

It's hard to imagine what would have happened to Edith had Skipper not come along. After he retired, he gently suggested that they shut Well Hall up and move to more affordable lodgings. Thus it was that Edith finally left her beloved home after twenty-three years on 2 February 1922. She wrote to Berta Ruck of her last thoughts on the place:

> 'When you were at Well Hall I used often on summer evenings to slip away from the table and go and look through the window at the rest of you finishing your desserts and your flirtations and your arguments amongst the flowers and fruits and bright glasses and think "This is how I shall see it all some day when I am not alive any more." Well, it won't be Well Hall I shall go back to now when the time comes for it died before I did and it is quite dead.'

Another person Edith said goodbye to was Alice Hoatson, something that many – including Hubert – thought would never happen. The mousy housekeeper, who had been the source of so much angst and confusion, went to visit her sister in Yorkshire and when she returned, quietly rented a flat in Blackheath with Mrs Evans, who had run the poultry farm at Well Hall during the war. Alice worked as a nurse as she faded into obscurity, continuing to pretend that Rosamund and John were her niece and nephew; she always lived for their next visit to her. Her memories of Edith were mixed, as she once described their turbulent relationship:

> 'She was, I think, without exception, the dearest, naughtiest, most cruel, most kindly, affectionate creature God ever sent into this world. One had ever the conviction she was a law unto herself, neither to hold nor to bind, yet never able to sleep until she had made confession and as far as possible, reparation for any unkindness or injustice she had shown during the day. And there were many such instances.'

The very last thing Edith did before giving up her key was to write her will. Edith specified that the copyright of her work was never to be sold. Skipper was the executor and she left her property to be divided between him, Iris and Paul. Edith hadn't forgotten how Hubert had ignored them in his will and so she did the same to his illegitimate children, Rosamund and John.

THE EXTRAORDINARY LIFE OF E. NESBIT

When Skipper metaphorically carried Edith over the threshold into their new home, it was the beginning of a new chapter for them both. The couple had converted two brick RAF huts overlooking a farm on Edith's beloved Kent coast. Although a fraction of the size of Well Hall, their new home was full of character; the longer building was christened the Long Boat and the squarer one the Jolly Boat, and the two buildings were connected with a passageway – jokingly referred to as the quarterdeck gangway or the Suez Canal. The huts had been used as stores and a photo lab during the war and lay between Dymchurch and New Romney just off Jefferstone Lane. Finally, Edith was to live in a property she owned in Kent, a place she had loved all her life, overlooking the Romney Marshes. Edith had brought Skipper to Dymchurch to recover after an illness and he too fell in love with the seaside village. They both found it quite beautiful with, 'the sound of the sea and the skylarks and the forever changing beauty of the marsh and the sky'. The retired couple were well looked after as they brought along their housekeeper from Well Hall, Olive Hill, who had become good friends with Edith. In a light-hearted, happy letter to a friend Edith describes her new house:

> '...our bungalow is only half built. So that where I should be sleeping, workmen are building... Most of the rooms are mere plane [plain] surfaces indicated by chalk lines on a cement floor. The rooms that are done are filled to overflowing with battens and quartering and matchboards and planks and doors... Shavings are knee-deep everywhere, and where there is nothing else there are carpenters' benches of far more than three dimensions.'

Edith relished pottering about supervising the home improvements, especially the chance to order her new husband around as he helped out. 'Edith designed and supervised the alterations – never was a big architect happier. Of course I was permitted to saw, drive in nails and such like,' wrote Skipper of the happy time. The turbulence of Edith's stormy life had come to a peaceful dock at last with her very own ship's captain. The fact that she was loved unconditionally and was able to love him back unselfconsciously gave Edith great peace. It released her, finally, from the longing for a stable male figure in her life that she had yearned for. In turn, there was no need to write children's stories anymore and instead she produced happy adult stories including her last novel *The Lark* (1922), a comic and light-hearted re-telling of her final years at Well Hall about two resourceful young women who turn a large, grand house into a florist and boarding house. She was delighted when readers told her it is 'jolly good stuff... rather to my surprise'. Edith described to a friend that these were 'the happiest years of my life':

> 'My own future – what there is of it – pleases me more and more. I am growing very fond of Mr Tucker, and I am never dull with him. And it is a great happiness to feel that some one else thinks that you are the happiness of his life. He deserves all the happiness in the world, for he is as good as gold.'

Chapter 20

The End

'The Skipper and I feel that we are old by some mistake.'

Edith Nesbit

Shakespeare believed that all the world's a stage, the men and women in it are merely players and that growing old is akin to infanthood. As an author known for her children's books, Edith agreed, as she wrote in *Wings and the Child or The Building of Magic Cities* (1913):

'For a middle-aged gentleman with a beard or a stout elderly lady with spectacles to move among other elderly and spectacled persons feeling that they are still children, and that the other elderly and spectacled ones are really grown-ups, seems thoroughly unreasonable, and therefore those who have never forgotten [their childhood] do not, as a rule, say anything about it. They just mingle with the other people, looking as grown-up as any one – but in their hearts they are only pretending to be grown-up: it is like acting in a charade. Time with his make-up box of lines and wrinkles, his skilful brush that paints out the tints and contours of youth, his supply of grey wigs and rounded shoulders and pillows for the waist, disguises the actors well enough, and they go through life together unsuspected...

'They will be easily pleased and easily hurt, and the grown-ups in grain will contemplate their pains and their pleasures with uncomprehending irritation.'

Now 64, Edith didn't feel her age. 'The Skipper and I feel that we are old by some mistake,' she wrote to Lord Dunsany. She still loved having children around her, often the offspring of her friends, and enjoyed reading the many letters she had received from her young fans from around the world. Her gift for making friends had been one of the greatest joys of her life and one of the very last people she met was Noël Coward who once wrote of her, 'She had… an unparalleled talent for evoking hot summer days in the English countryside.' After a holiday in Dymchurch in 1922, the young playwright (he had just started in the theatre) loved it so much that he bought a cottage with his mother next to the Star Inn at St Mary's, not far from Edith's home. When he realised that he was living close to one of his childhood heroes, he went to visit her. 'I burst in upon her. She was absolutely charming. From then on we became friends,' he wrote. It's not difficult to imagine how delighted Edith was to meet the erudite young writer and they saw a great deal of each other for the last two years of her life, chatting over tea at each other's places, despite more than forty years between them. '[I] found her as firm, as nice, and as humorous as her books had led me to expect,' wrote Coward. 'The Skipper, her husband, was a grand old man who loved her and guarded her devotedly.' Coward amused Edith with the story of how as a child he would regularly save up all his pocket money to buy second-hand copies of the *Strand Magazine* so he could read her stories that were serialised. 'She was the only children's writer – of recent times – who was first rate; she had a real sense of humour.' Once, he even stole a coral necklace from one of his mother's friends and pawned it so he could buy one of Edith's books. His favourite novel was *Five Children and It*. 'She is unspeakably underrated,' he once said:

> 'She was a strange case of being a real Bohemian – the most genuine Bohemian I have ever seen. Money, for instance, didn't matter to her. She didn't seem to mind being poor. I loved her because she was so far from being a "sweet old lady"! She was very acid. Yes, she had an astringent tongue – a witty and amusing tongue. She got cross with me sometimes. I didn't mind that. I remember her getting very cross once about my being late for tea or something. She couldn't stand people being late for meals.'

He recalled that she made no bones about the fact that she didn't like his mother when she met her and Coward admired her all the more for her honesty, asking her opinion on a couple of scripts for his early plays, 'She was encouraging about my work… but she was a severe critic. She didn't know much about the theatre, but she had a strong sense of character.' Although Coward was only 21 at the time he met Edith, knowing her and remembering her wit and humour made an impression on him for the rest of his life. He bought some of her furniture (and was delighted when she threw in a rocking chair for free) and when he died, there was a copy of her *The Enchanted Castle* at his bedside. He was the only person in her life who she allowed to call her Nesbit:

'I am reading again through all the dear E. Nesbits and they seem to be more charming and evocative than ever. It is strange that after half a century I still get so much pleasure from them. Her writing is so light and unforced, her humour is so sure and her narrative quality so strong that the stories, which I know backwards, rivet me as much now as they did when I was a little boy. Even more so in one way because I can now enjoy her actual talent and her extraordinary power of describing hot summer days in England in the beginning years of the century. All the pleasant memories of my own childhood jump at me from the pages... E. Nesbit knew all the things that stay in the mind, all the happy treasures. I suppose she, of all the writers I have ever read, has given me over the years the most complete satisfaction...'

Coward introduced her to other new friends including the writer G.B. Stern; even in the middle of rural Kent, Edith still attracted around her an arty set. During her years of holidays at Dymchurch she had become friends with the Thorndike family and picked up the acquaintance again. Russell Thorndike was a novelist of the Dr Syn mysteries set in the area, and was the brother of a well-known actress of the time. The irrepressible Dame Sibyl Thorndike was a member of the Royal Shakespeare Company and starred in films with Laurence Olivier and Marilyn Monroe. Sybil's eldest son recalls going to see Edith in the summer of 1922 and being welcomed by the small, stocky Skipper, whom he described as almost a caricature of an old sailor as they were welcomed by his words:

'"Avast there, me hearties! ... avast there, me hearties!" He would shout as [we] drove up to the bungalow. "Come aboard. Tea's ready in the Long Boat but Madam's titivating herself in the Jolly Boat.'

The summer of 1922 was to be Edith's last healthy one. Her lungs had been irreparably damaged after years of smoking and over the winter the cough, bronchitis and asthma she suffered permanently became worse. The Skipper became her full-time carer along with Olive Hill. Disinterested in food, Edith lost a great deal of weight and joked that her curvy Rubenesque figure had become a slim Pre-Raphaelite. Her brown curls had finally succumbed to grey and her once-tanned face and arms had faded to pale. Too weak to hold a pen, she dictated letters to Olive and sat propped up in bed overlooking her beloved Romney Marsh. But as the warmer weather of summer 1923 came, so did an old friend to cheer her up. Berta Ruck had first met Edith as a teenager, when she was a friend of Iris at the Slade art school. Now an established novelist, wife and mother, Berta bumped into Iris in London and when she learned Edith was ill, Berta was keen to see her again. They wrote and Beta went to visit Edith. After missing her train, Berta arrived at a different time than planned. 'You're very late, girl!' Edith greeted her crossly. Quick as a whip, Berta replied 'Fifteen years...' Edith loved the quip and the two became friends again. They had lost touch after a quarrel some fifteen years before but Berta had never forgotten the older woman's mentoring and Edith had always remained fond of her. 'I always took an interest in your work and believed in it and thought you would do great things,' she told her. Berta in turn showed Edith what she was working on and Edith took care to read it properly and make considered suggestions. 'You know I think that to write anything less than one's very very best is the unpardonable sin,' she told Berta, writing that poetry should be 'simple, sonorous and ... sincere'. Edith impressed upon Berta the importance of writing what she wanted to write rather than what she thought would sell. 'She took more trouble over me than anybody,' Berta remembered:

> 'As a lanky girl, I used to sit, quite literally, amongst scattered sheets of manuscript paper at her feet... I wish I could convey to you her patience in listening to my screeds, her generosity in praising any phrase or bit of description that she could approve – her incomparable frankness... I can hear her now, saying brusquely of some such passage, "Won't do, Berta! Won't do".'

Although Edith's body was failing, her mind remained as sharp as her eyes that pierced from behind big round glasses. Berta continued:

> 'We had some wonderful talks, though now she lay always on her sofa, instead of moving about the room as she talked. She had the same gestures with her hands, small, and very alive hands, that I remembered sunburnt and brown from her much rowing and swimming. They were now strangely white, the sunburn had faded, but there stood out the freckles that she had acquired in long ago summers of the Nineteenth Century... However thin and wasted in body, her hair grown grey, the gaiety of her spirit still shone through her eyes.'

Edith's sense of humour hadn't left her either; for one visit, Berta bought some flowers from Harrods; red roses, carnations, freesias and narcissus. She, along with Olive Hill, opened the boxes slowly and carefully so Edith could enjoy the anticipation. In fact, her childish delight enjoyed it so much that she sighed and wished they could all be packed up and opened again – before cheekily pointing at Berta and accusing her:

> '"Berta! Those flowers. You bought them now, really, instead of for my funeral? You thought, why not let her have them while she can enjoy them? Didn't you?"
> '"Yes," I snapped. "I did."
> '"So sensible," she said, satisfied, and sniffed at her red carnations.'

Her re-acquaintance with Berta meant a great deal to Edith, and they would often write – Edith dictating her letters to Olive, signing off as 'Once Duchess of Dymchurch'. Edith felt there was still so much of life to explore and she must have been frustrated that she could no longer have such freedom:

> 'For the people who keep their wits and their health, the human span of life is far too short. What things there are still to see and to do, and to think and to be and to grow into and to grow out of!'

In another letter, she joked about almost passing away:

> 'I did nearly die last week and I assure you that the hitch in the arrangements was no fault of mine… better luck next time.'

Her illness was causing Edith great discomfort, with a constant cough and the pain of her duodenal ulcer. 'It's a long business and I am getting very tired of it,' she wrote. 'But just when I hope the end may be in sight I get a little better and realise miserably that I've got to go on with it a bit longer.' The natural world had always sustained Edith, and writers throughout her career from Oscar Wilde to Noël Coward had acclaimed her keen eye for nature. And so the countryside would provide a comfort to her in old age as she gazed out of the window (a friend helped raise her four-poster bed for a better view). Edith wrote:

> 'I have everything to make me happy except health, kindest and most loving nursing and care. My bedroom is 20ft x 15ft, a four-post bed like a golden shrine and a view of about 8 miles of marsh bounded by the little lovely hills of Kent.'

THE END

She continued to delight in her visitors and her family would go to see her often along with others from her past including her old admirers, Noel Griffith and Edward Andrade. Life came full circle when Edith's oldest friend from childhood, Ada Breakell, came to stay from London for a month.

Although Edith maintained her social life, she had plenty of time for reflection. Surrounded with shelves crammed with the books she so loved to read, and her familiar favourite pieces of furniture and knick-knacks from Well Hall, she enjoyed remembering all the parties and the people of those years ago. She loved looking through a scrapbook that a friend made for Skipper's birthday, which had been carefully made by pasting in highlights of her career and she reflected on all she had achieved. She couldn't help but retain a tinge of regret that she was known as a children's author rather than a poet:

> 'I'm so glad when anyone likes my poetry. It is really what I should naturally have done, that and no prose, if I had not to write for a living.'

During the long, sleepless nights when she gazed out at the stars she turned her mind to her childhood and thought of her brothers, and their promise as children to always remember each other when they saw the Great Bear constellation. Iris recalled one of their last conversations, when she asked her mother if she would live her life over again. Edith said she would, every single minute of it, because it had 'all been so passionately interesting'.

Edith refused to feel sad about being old but welcomed the end, gallantly fending off death as she imagined herself as a queen lying on a throne-like four-poster bed covered with roses (perhaps the morphine talking). During the last year of her life she lived in constant pain and by December 1923 she was bedridden. In a letter to Berta Ruck she wrote 'I do really get less and less alive.' Yet although her face was ashen, she was cheered by her surroundings in the Jolly Boat and her eyes still burned bright; less than a month before she died, Edith continued to write letters and was attempting to write a poem that was in her head. Her final words to Berta were:

> 'Good bye, my dear. Whenever you think of me do not forget to think how much happiness your loving kindness has given me and how you have helped my last, long months. I really think the door will open soon now and I may be able to scurry through at last.'

In the end there were three serious illnesses that killed Edith; bronchial trouble in her lungs from years of smoking, heart problems and an ulcer. Her final four days were agonising. Her children were sent for and on 4 May 1924 Paul and Iris were by her side, with her housekeeper and friend Olive Hill, a nurse and the Skipper. Edith's hair streaked with grey was tied in two plaits, a nod to her forever girlishness, her skin pale as ivory and her dark eyes full of pain; she died in the arms of Iris.

Of course, being Edith, there would have to be some twist to her death. Her wild imagination for horror and ghost stories meant her secret fear had been she would be buried alive as her grandfather had almost been. So an artery was cut to prove her life had finally come to a close. Sadly, and tenderly, the Skipper fashioned a simple wooden panel carved with her name, her lucky sign of a four-leaf clover, and the words:

> 'E Nesbit, Mrs Bland-Tucker, Poet & Author
> Died 4 May 1924, aged 65'

The Skipper carried out this old naval custom in place of a headstone at his wife's grave as she was buried under an elm tree at the local church of St Mary's in the Marsh. He would later write:

> 'Above all let us bless her for that view of gentle humans which is like a ray of sunlight through all she writes and gives her narrative a merry grace of movement. It is this, perhaps, which among many other excellent qualities most endears her to childish readers and to many others. We feel, even in these simple pieces, a sound, sane, cheerful and hearty outlook on life, a firm hold on the human condition and yet a playful and delicate imagination.'

Edith's funeral was attended by her family, the local villagers and her closest friends including Noel Griffith and Edward Andrade. It is not recorded if Alice Hoatson came. Edith's body was surrounded by a mass of her favourite flowers sent from around the country from friends old and new such as Berta Ruck, Marshall Steele, Bower Marsh, Elsa Courlander and Noël Coward. Edith died as one of the greatest children's authors to have ever lived, beloved by her fans from around the world. As for her friends and family, she would never be forgotten, no matter what else they thought of her: 'E. Nesbit was like nobody else. She was certainly one of the most remarkable women of her time, by sheer force of character, even apart from her literary output,' remembered one of her former lovers Gerald Gould.

Obituaries were published in newspapers around the world from Bloemfontein in South Africa in the *Farmer's Weekly*, to the *Daily Times* in

THE END

British Columbia in Canada to the *Evening Post* in New York, *New Zealand Herald* in Wellington to *The Chronicle* in Adelaide and *The Worker* in Brisbane. Strangely, some including *The Times* in London, wrote of her as Elizabeth Nesbit.

When an author dies, a great sadness is that they will never again write anything else. Today, Edith's admirers – both young and old, from Britain and around the world – must be content with the 100 or so books, collections of poems and other publications she left behind. Perhaps we can all find pleasure in re-reading her work, too, as one of her young fans Joy Ridley of Kensington Square in London, wrote.

> 'Dear Mrs Nesbit
> 'I have read nearly all of your beautiful books for children, and love every one of them, but the one I love the very best of all is *The Phoenix and the Carpet*. Please do you think one day you could be so very kind as to write another book about Cyril, Anthea, Robert and Jane with the Phoenix… Daddy gave it to me last Christmas…I have read it twelve times since then. When the Phoenix goes away it makes me feel so sad that I go back to the beginning again…
> 'With lots of love from Joy Ridley'

Edith Nesbit often liked to have the final word, so it is perhaps appropriate to close with a quote from the last book she wrote, *The Lark* (1922). The light-hearted tale features two girls, one an optimist (Edith?) and one a realist (Alice Hoatson?). The ever-sunny Jane is determined to see the best of a bad situation and always looks on the bright side of life and perhaps her words sum up Edith's approach to life, work and what lies beyond death:

> 'Everything that's happening to us – yes, everything – is to be regarded as a lark. See? This is my last word. This. Is. Going. To. Be. A. Lark.'

Postscript

The Skipper continued to live in the Long Boat and the Jolly Boat, and became known as 'the Father of Jepson' because of all his good work for the community there. He set up a social club for local entertainment, volunteered at the hospital in Folkestone and organised a school bus for local children. A year after Edith's death, Rosamund compiled a collection of some of the last stories she had worked on, including the one she had written with the Skipper called 'Tammy Lee's Jack', and published it in 1925 as *The Five of Us – and Madeline* (T. Fisher Unwin). In the autumn of 1932, Rosamund came to live with the Skipper to give him a hand – by now he was in his late seventies – and the housekeeper Olive Hill moved out the following year. Rosamund knew he didn't like being looked after but she did all she could to make his life more comfortable as he wasn't really well enough to live on his own. Inspired by her mother's success, Rosamund completed her own novel in 1934 whilst living at the Long Boat. Called *The Man in the Stone House* and published by J. Miles it is about a woman who falls for an older man on the Romney Marsh. A year later, on 17 May 1935, the same month Edith had died, Rosamund held Skipper's hand as he passed away aged 79 after a stroke a previous week. His funeral was at the same church as Edith's, St Mary's, and he was probably buried with Edith although, sadly, there is no record of his grave. Today, a miniature steam railway runs past their former home as it gently chugs its way between Hythe and Dungeness, a fitting reminder of its most famous resident.

Although Edith's stories are full of happy children, sadly her own family wasn't destined for a joyful life. Paul, the eldest, had the saddest time of it. His recollections of his mother were kind and fond, but the man was too gentle for this world: after retreating from his overbearing wife Gertrude into his hobbies of gardening and cars, it all became too much for him and he committed suicide aged 60 by poisoning himself on 9 October 1940. Iris continued to work as a dressmaker while her daughter Pandora became a famous ballerina with Anna Pavlova's dance company. Pandora had a son, Max and she also adopted a daughter, called Fern, but when Pandora was tragically killed in a car accident in the 1950s, Iris cared for them until she died. Rosamund's husband Clifford Sharp became an alcoholic and the disease eventually killed him after an unhappy marriage. Sadly, Rosamund lived out the rest of her days destitute and died aged 63 on 8 March 1950 in Golders Green in north London. John was bright enough to be accepted into Cambridge University and fortunately was given the means to do so (in secret) by George Bernard Shaw. He eventually became an expert in bacteriology and lived in Cairo, working for the Egyptian government in the late 1930s. Here he was regarded as a quiet, serious, reflective person who learned Arabic – but with a streak of his mother's fun as he was a fabulous dancer who always joined in with silly party games. He eventually came back to England and died at St Bart's Hospital on 11 May 1946 after suffering TB the previous year. Rosamund went to his funeral at Golder's Green Crematorium and his ashes were scattered at Payne's Hill. Married twice, he was survived by two daughters who went to Cambridge and Oxford.

And what of the magnificent Well Hall? Sadly, it seemed to die with its last occupant, lying empty until 1929 when the Borough of Woolwich bought it. It went to rack and ruin – the gardens became overgrown, the walls crumbled and even Edith's beloved wooden boat was half-sunk in the moat. The house was eventually demolished in March 1931 because it was too expensive to maintain. There was a promise that a library would be built with an emphasis on loaning children's books, but this fitting tribute was never to be. Instead, the grounds were made into a park, the Well Hall Pleasaunce, and in 1988 Greenwich Council and English Heritage gloriously restored the Tudor garden's brick walls, replanted flowerbeds and replaced fruit trees. A plaque records where Edith's house once stood. The moat and medieval bridge still remain, along with the original garden walls and one of the towering black poplars at the entrance to the park. The only building that exists from Edith's time is the farmer's Tudor Barn, formerly an art gallery and now a restaurant and pub. Other careful additions to the Well Hall grounds include a children's playground and three striking statues carved from sweet chestnut, depicting three of her most famous characters: the Psammead (*Five Children and It*), the Phoenix (*The Phoenix and the Carpet*) and the Dragon (*The Book of Beasts*). These were unveiled on 9 May 2013 by Jacqueline Wilson, author of *Four Children and It*, who was inspired by Edith to become a writer. Another addition is Edith Nesbit Walk, which lies between Well Hall Pleasaunce and the railway line. Many of these updates to the park were suggested by the Edith Nesbit Society, which remains closely connected to Well Hall. Founded in 1996, the Society aims to celebrate the life and work of Edith through talks and publications, of which it produces on a regular basis – www.edithnesbit.co.uk.

Chapter 21

The Afterlife: Re-Telling E. Nesbit's Stories

The Railway Children is Edith's most adapted novel and the actress most associated with it is Jenny Agutter, who played Roberta in the 1968 BBC television series before she made the role of Bobbie her own in the iconic 1970 film and, exactly thirty years later, Mother in the 2000 version with Richard Attenborough as the Old Gentleman. A life member of the Edith Nesbit Society, Jenny Agutter says that she had no idea at the time the impact the film would make, and more than forty years later she finds that people are still enthusiastic to talk to her about it. Because of her happy memories of filming the story as a young actress, she was pleased to be a part of the 2000 production:

> 'I have enjoyed working on *The Railway Children* and loved the chance to play Mother, which I always felt was about Nesbit herself, just as Roberta was also created from Edith's memories of her childhood in Kent, living close to the railways. A costume designer pointed out to me that red flannel petticoats would have been worn in the late 1800s when Edith was a child rather than 1905 when the book was published.
>
> 'I became particularly interested in Edith Nesbit's life after reading *A Woman of Passion* [by Julia Briggs] and at one point was trying to put together a film based on her and the people surrounding her.
>
> 'Her ability to see the world clearly through the eyes of a child has endeared her to generation after generation and her strong sense of morality makes her stories as relevant now as they have ever been.
>
> 'I am sure *The Railway Children* will continue to delight audiences of all ages for many years to come.'

Similarly, Bernard Cribbins, who played Perks in the 1970 film, is still regularly approached by people of different generations who tell him *The Railway Children* is their favourite film:

> 'It is a lovely story and Lionel Jeffries told it well. I enjoyed it then and I am still enjoying it now all those years later.
>
> 'Jenny Agutter was, what, 17 then? She and the kids were a delight. The film was great fun to do. It is a lovely story. Perks is a nice gentleman, a caring father figure and it was a very good part altogether. I have very happy memories of making the film. The location in Yorkshire was an absolute joy and the railway people up there were most helpful. My wife and I were staying at Bolton Abbey and I used to finish the day's shooting, come back for a drink and then spend the evening fly fishing and maybe catch a trout – or not.'

Cribbins remembers the royal premiere at the Saville Theatre, London:

> 'We were in costume and sitting behind Princess Margaret and Prince Edward, who was quite young then. He turned around at one point and did a double take when he saw me – the same person who was 12 foot up on the screen. It was a lovely moment.'

In 2014 Bernard Cribbins was reunited after forty-four years with Jenny Agutter and Gary Warren, who played Peter, to receive the J.M. Barrie Award in recognition of his lifetime of work for generations of children. He was awarded an OBE in 2011.

Oakworth Station in West Yorkshire was the location used in the film; it is on the route of the Keighley and Worth Valley Railway (KWVR) that was set up by a group of enthusiasts two years before filming to restore steam trains to the area (some of the volunteers appeared as extras in the film). The station became famous after the film was released and the steam trains now carry 100,000 passengers a year. In 2018 the railway will celebrate its 50th anniversary www.kwvr.co.uk.

Perhaps the most famous re-telling in recent times of *The Railway Children* is the Olivier Award-winning stage show featuring a real steam train weighing some 60 tonnes. Written by Mike Kenny and directed by Damian Cruden, the production was originally staged in York in 2008 at the National Railway Museum by York Theatre Royal. In 2010, the production transferred to Waterloo

Station in the former Eurostar terminal. Returning to London in 2011, it won the Olivier Award for Best Entertainment before opening in Toronto in Canada. It came back to London, this time to King's Cross Station in a purpose-built thousand-seat theatre, featuring a stage built around a real train track. The final show was 8 January 2017.

'Edith Nesbit feels like a modern writer,' says the writer of the show, Mike Kenny:

> 'The book is about people making the decision to help others and recognising why that's important. I think this is what touches people. Small acts of kindness become almost a political statement.'

Kenny used the railway as an additional character, heavy with metaphoric meaning:

> 'The railway was the internet of the day – it changed people's lives through communication and by making the world seem smaller. The railway takes away the children's father, and then brings him back – both symbolically when the children play on it and have adventures and also later, in reality, through the old gentleman.'

Caroline Harker played the role of Mother for five years – one of only two actors to be associated with the production for its entirety. Her step-daughter Louise Calf played the part of Phyllis in Kings Cross twice during its run. Says Harker:

> 'It was a production on a huge scale. Everything was large: the space of the theatre – especially at Waterloo under the great glass roof – the train, which was on a correct-sized train track, and the sound – it virtually blew us away when the train puffed into the station. As an actor it felt like we were Hornby toy people, we realised how small we were compared with the scaled-up set and the train. You get that goosebump feeling immediately as you are transported back to 1906.' As part of her research Harker visited Edith's final home and re-traced her steps in London. 'Sometimes during the show at Kings Cross, I'd imagine Edith and Bernard Shaw setting out from there, on one of their long walks. I wanted to do her justice, especially as the book means so much to so many people. I would have quite liked to play Mother as Edith – long

flowing scarves and a fag on the go!' [Harker sums up the story's success] 'I think it is because the story doesn't patronise at all and the dialogue between the three children crosses all generations and nations. It's a selfless tale, fondly written and it shows faith in people. Everyone is good inside really.'

David Baron played the part of the Old Gentleman with Caroline Harker at Waterloo. An actor, writer and lyricist, Baron has had a thirty year association with *The Railway Children* – almost by accident and despite not having read it as a child nor seen the 1970 film. He wrote the lyrics to the first musical version in the 1980s and its success attracted interest in the West End. In 1987 the Mercury Theatre in Colchester asked David to write a new production to be staged as a play without songs, and it had a sell-out Christmas run. Almost thirty years later, Baron auditioned for the role of the Old Gentlemen for the new staging of *The Railway Children* at Waterloo. 'I went along and I think they liked the fact that I knew the play and I took it seriously. I knew it wasn't just a children's story.' At 80 years of age it was to be his last role and he was thrilled when the show won an Olivier Award in 2011.

The *Five Children* series has become the second-most adapted of all of Edith's work. One of the most acclaimed is the award-winning novel *Five Children on the Western Front* by Kate Saunders (2014, Faber & Faber). 'Edith Nesbit has inspired everybody who came after her who writes for children. All good children's writing sounds a bit like Nesbit,' says Saunders, whose sequel follows the family during the First World War and is exceptional for capturing the tone and characterisation of the original story while offering a warm and wise reflection on the horrors the children are forced to face. As the generation who lived through 1914 to 1918, their innocence is lost forever. 'When my publisher asked me to write something about World War I, I couldn't resist writing about the five children and the Psammead,' says Saunders:

> 'The Psammead is a very, very good device for explaining about the Kaiser to modern kids and I knew I could be trusted to write about magic if I wrote about it through the children.'

She was heavily influenced by the final part of the original trilogy, *The Story of the Amulet*:

> 'It wasn't Nesbit's best one but I adapted one of the chapters for the Prologue, when the Professor is seen in the future. Edith Nesbit

didn't know World War I was about to happen when she wrote *Five Children* – and neither did the character of the Professor.'

Saunders didn't set out to emulate Nesbit's narrative voice:

'I was absolutely gobsmacked when the book was a success. If anyone has gone from my book and tried Nesbit, then that is lovely. Isn't it brilliant?

'E. Nesbit is the mother of children's writing because she was the first author who became celebrated for speaking to children as an equal and not patronising them. She had a very vivid remembrance of childhood and never talked down to her readers. Her particular use of English and the way she transposed ideas and jokes is friendly, witty and sophisticated. She also introduced the idea of low magic – what would happen if you fell asleep in your wings and couldn't fly home? That clash between the real and the magical is funny and children really like that, and so do I.

'100 years later Edith Nesbit's voice is still here and I'm all in favour of more attention being drawn to her. She is endlessly fascinating.'

Tragically, the two authors became inextricably linked when Saunders suffered the loss of her son, who committed suicide a year before she started writing *Five Children on the Western Front*. The book's deeply touching finale could only have been written by a mother who has lost a son.

A totally different adaptation of *Five Children and It* is the 2004 Hollywood film starring Kenneth Branagh as the new character of Uncle Albert and an animatronic puppet of It made by Jim Henson's Creature Shop, voiced by Eddie Izzard. Set slightly later than the original story, in 1914, it follows the five children as they are evacuated during the First World War. Kenneth Branagh says:

'E. Nesbit makes a leap in the imagination. [Her writing] has a surreal quality that she was rather pioneering about in her own way. It was a different kind of comedy from the world of Lewis Carroll. And also it was very, very outdoorsy, very adventure-led and very physical without being so hearty and male that it excludes girls. She somehow managed to create a very particular world that you have enormous amounts of fun [in] and you could be daft but it wasn't too soft. Somehow she creates a place where children can really be let off the leash.'

Perhaps the best-loved adaptation of *Five Children and It* is the 1991 BBC six-part television series (called *The Sand-fairy* when it was shown in the United States). Although this Psammead only has two eyes (that are firmly positioned on his head rather than on stalks), he looks exactly as the reader might have imagined and is a practically perfect mixture of the lovable and cantankerous. Who could forget the wheezing sound he makes as he puffs up his belly and makes the children's wishes come true? Helen Creswell wrote the series and followed it up a year later with a novel called *The Return of the Psammead*, which she also adapted for the screen.

In the United States, Edward Eager applied Edith's approach to a series of novels about American children in the 1950s, the most well-known of which is *Half-Magic;* four siblings unearth various magical talismans and cope with the unpredictable results of granted wishes.

Most recently, A.S. Byatt's *The Children's Book* (2009) is a dense, intellectual re-telling of Edith and Hubert's bohemian life, which has won critical acclaim.

Chapter 22

Harry Potter

'I love E. Nesbit.'

J.K. Rowling OBE

The Harry Potter series of seven novels about an ordinary boy who becomes a wizard is one of the most famous contemporary children's stories. The series has sold more than 450 million copies around the world and translated into 80 languages, with eight blockbuster films inspired by the books.

Where did J.K. Rowling gain her inspiration? Perhaps some of it may have come from Edith Nesbit. 'She's the children's writer with whom I most identify,' said Rowling in an interview.

> '[Edith Nesbit] said, "By some lucky chance, I remember exactly how I felt and thought at 11." That struck a chord with me. *The Story of the Treasure Seekers* was a breakthrough children's book. Oswald is such a very real narrator, at a time when most people were writing morality tales for children.'

Edith was one of the first writers to mix real magic with ordinary children, and Rowling uses this technique brilliantly as the basis for her novels. Harry is an ordinary boy who has extraordinary experiences, just as Edith's heroes and heroines do – from the five children who discover the Psammead, to Eldred and Elfrida Arden in *The House of Arden*. In *The Phoenix and the Carpet*, Jane says, 'I wish they taught magic at school.'

Further, both Edith and Rowling's extraordinary imaginations have created some of the most vivid animal creatures in children's literature – from Edith's magic mouldiwarp mole in *The House of Arden* (complete with old-fashioned Kentish accent) to J.K. Rowling's niffler, a bit like a duck-billed platypus who loves anything shiny. These women were inspired by the creatures of myths and legends and wrote about the same type of magical beasts, including dragons, hippogriffs, chimeras and, of course, phoenix.

To accompany the Harry Potter saga, Rowling wrote *Fantastic Beasts and Where to Find Them* (2001). It's a spoof textbook that explains her magical creatures in detail, meant for the students of Harry's boarding school, Hogwarts School of Witchcraft and Wizardry. The book was written for charity and was made into a film in 2016.

Edith's *The Book of Beasts* appeared as a story in the *Strand Magazine* in March 1899. When a small boy called Lionel suddenly becomes king, he discovers a peculiar book in the royal library buzzing with mythical creatures that come alive when he turns each page. He accidentally releases a great Red Dragon, which guzzles an entire football team, an orphanage and even the Parliament.

Rowling's dragons are just as fearful and an essential part of the Harry Potter series, intrinsic to the wizarding world. They are the most famous of magical beasts, and Hogwart's school motto is translated from Latin into 'never tickle a sleeping dragon'. Harry's foe is Draco Malfoy, whose name is derived from the Greek word for dragon, and dragon heartstrings help make wands. We first meet a Rowling dragon in book one, *The Philosopher's Stone*, when Hagrid the giant hatches a dragon called Norbert, whom he later humorously discovers is a girl and re-christens her Norberta. One of the most thrilling episodes featuring dragons is book four, *The Goblet of Fire*, in the exciting Triwizard Tournament, the international competition in which Harry represents his school. The First Task is for the four contestants to bravely take a golden dragon's egg from one of the four varieties: the Hungarian Horntail, Common Welsh Green, Swedish Short-Snout and Chinese Fireball – the latter is red, the same colour as in Edith's *The Book of Beasts*. Enormous in size, fire pours from their fanged mouths (some can shoot from forty feet), with horns, spikes and roars that can only be controlled by seven or eight wizards each.

Like Harry Potter, Edith's Lionel is clever enough to work out a solution to counter the dangerous beasts and sources a manticora, the creature from Greek myth with the head of a man and the body of a lion. Unfortunately, the manticora is swiftly digested (somewhat humorously) by the Red Dragon. J.K. Rowling's manticore looks the same but is terrifying, and is one of the most dangerous of her beasts (it is briefly mentioned in book three, *The Prisoner of Azkaban*, as being capable of savaging someone).

When Lionel opens *The Book of Beasts* again, he comes across a beautiful white winged horse: the sweet-natured Hippogriff. Edith's version of the mythical beast differs from the ones of ancient Greece and Rome: Rowling's hippogriffs in *The Prisoner of Azkaban*, are in line with the traditional idea of half-horse, half-eagle. Proud in nature they have cruel beaks and sharp talons. Harry is introduced to a Buckbeak who is a pet of his friend and teacher, the giant Hagrid. The hippogriff is temperamental and must be flattered and bowed down to (unlike Edith's who is bashful at praise). Eyes are also significant: Buckbeak has orange eyes that Harry must stare out to gain the creature's trust while Lionel's has the 'most beautiful eyes in the world'. Perhaps Edith's hippogriff is more closely related to Rowling's winged horses as seen in book four, *The Goblet of Fire*?

Either way, both authors use hippogriffs as a catalyst for their plots. It is the hippogriff that ultimately saves Lionel and his kingdom from danger by flying higher and faster than the Red Dragon, tricking him back into *The Book of Beasts*. Harry Potter uses Buckbeak's powerful flying skills to rescue his godfather, Sirius Black, from the deadly Dementors. Sirius and Buckbeak continue into the next book as outlaws together: the hippogriff is renamed Witherwings to protect his true identity, proving himself loyal as well as brave – just as Lionel's hippogriff is.

Faithfulness is a characteristic shared by another favourite beast of Edith and J.K. Rowling. Both authors dedicated a book to the creature; *The Phoenix and the Carpet* (1904) and the fifth of the Harry Potter series, *The Order of the Phoenix*. Edith's phoenix appears in the follow-up to *Five Children and It* when Jane, Anthea, Cyril, Robert and the Lamb discover an egg in their bedroom fireplace. 'The size of an eagle… its head finely crested with a beautiful plumage, its neck covered with feathers of a gold colour...' More refined than the Psammead (the Phoenix is unfailingly polite), the creature is somewhat haughty and gets physically tired like the sand fairy. The Phoenix is much more visible than the Psammead as he lives with the children and although it can't grant wishes it works in tandem with a magic carpet that transports the children across the world. Adventures include collecting treasures in India and mistakenly bringing home 199 Persian cats.

Adventure is the order of the day for Harry Potter in the fifth book when he joins a group of wizards known as the Order of the Phoenix to battle their deadly enemy, Voldemort. Harry came across a phoenix in the first book, *The Chamber of Secrets*, when he meets his headmaster's bird called Fawkes (is this name a coincidence, when Edith's children meet their phoenix shortly after Guy Fawkes night? Or perhaps it is simply a play on the bird's association with fire). Fiercely loyal to Dumbledore, Fawkes saves Harry's life.

On the subject of magic, another crossover is that both J.K. Rowling and Edith use the concept of turning children into animals – known to Harry Potter as animagi. In *The House of Arden,* brother and sister Eldred and Elfrida turn into white cats, for example. *The House of Arden* also explores the idea of time travel as a method of altering the future, a theme common between Nesbit and

Rowling. In Harry Potter book three, *The Prisoner of Azkaban*, Hermione uses a Time-Turner hourglass to go back to the past and save Buckbeak the hippogriff from being executed. *The House of Arden* sees Eldred and Elfrida go back in time to meet their ancestors and famous historical figures such as Sir Walter Raleigh to restore the fortunes of their once-great family. The lovely images of photographs that magically depict moving scenes in the children's homemade dark room evoke Rowling's wizarding newspaper, *The Daily Prophet*. Both authors perfectly capture a child's imagination and excitement. Being invisible is another wish common amongst children – and, again, Rowling and Nesbit demonstrate how in touch they are with their readers as both use the device in their stories. Harry Potter's invisibility cloak is vital to his adventures, and in *The House of Arden* and its sequel, *Harding's Luck*, Edith's characters become invisible as they travel through time.

Edith Nesbit and J.K. Rowling wrote about ordinary children who experience extraordinary adventures. These children are sometimes loners, such as Harry Potter or Lionel in *The Book of Beasts* who both have their lives changed overnight: Lionel becomes king because his long-lost ancestor turns into a wizard. Harry is the son of wizards. Both boys suddenly find themselves in an alien environment and must use their good characteristics of strength, gumption and common sense to overcome dangerous creatures and foolish grownups. Young readers are left in no doubt that these authors are on their side, with characters that have become dear to children despite the fact that they were written more than 100 years apart.

Chapter 23

An E. Nesbit for the Twenty-First Century

'I've bonded with her.'

Jacqueline Wilson is one of the world's best-loved contemporary children's authors. As the writer of *Four Children and It*, she has won multiple awards, was made a dame for her services to literature and was the Children's Laureate from 2005 to 2007. She has sold more than 40 million books in the UK and has been translated into 30 languages.

Wilson cites Edith Nesbit as her inspiration and there are remarkable parallels between the two women:

> 'For many years I didn't make any money from my books. My version of E. Nesbit's birthday cards was writing stories for magazines, which was frustrating as I couldn't write what I wanted to. I had my young daughter, Emma, to bring up and I was married to a man who believed it was my task to cook three meals a day and iron his shirts.
>
> 'I understand exactly what E. Nesbit was talking about when she described her children crying as she was pegging away with some commercial work, and I share her frustration with publishers. I've bonded with her.'

Just like Edith, Wilson has a prolific output. Now the author of more than 100 books, early in her career she would write an astounding 10,000 words of commercial fiction and 5,000 words of her own novels each week while Emma was at school. 'That is such a lot to do,' Wilson reflects, remembering how in those days she would buy buns with white sticky icing and a cherry on top for herself and Emma whenever she sold a story, just like the character of Mother did in *The Railway Children*. And, like Edith, Wilson would buy herself a piece of silver jewellery, often a ring, when a book was published:

'As a child and young person I didn't have jewellery that I liked, and I particularly loved the idea of the sound of Edith's bangles jangling up her arm.'

Both Edith and Wilson have pushed the boundaries of children's fiction because their characters are incredibly realistic, sometimes uncomfortably so. Edith's children – shock horror – were shown to argue, break things, get messy and generally engage in a lifestyle completely against the Victorian seen-and-not-heard ideal. Wilson too refuses to depict perfect families and instead writes about orphans, divorced parents, dysfunctional adults, step-siblings, half-brothers and half-sisters.

Wilson grew up as a lonely, only child in a small flat and, like Edith, remembers exactly what it is like to be a young. 'Ask me what I did two weeks ago and I'll have no idea but ask me what my life was like at ten or 12 and I remember vividly,' says Wilson, whose powerful memory is all the more impressive because her mother carelessly disposed of her diaries and juvenilia:

'I left home at 17 to work in Scotland [as a journalist on *Jackie* magazine in Dundee for D.C. Thomson, which now publishes *The Official Jacqueline Wilson Mag*]. When I came home a few months later at Christmas, it wasn't my bedroom anymore. My mother collected dolls and had made my room into a sort of doll museum, at the same time getting rid of my dolls, my diaries and all my writing that were in the top drawer. She only kept a few schoolbooks. I wish she hadn't done that. My daughter Emma is now 50 but I still have everything she ever had, from a postcard she wrote me a few months ago to all her writings and drawings.'

Wilson was six years old when she first came across Edith Nesbit's work, after being given a copy of *The Story of the Treasure Seekers*:

'I can still remember how I felt when I read Oswald's opening lines about introducing your characters clearly. I thought, "yes! That's exactly what I think".

'Instantly I recognised the book has a real child's voice and attitude but in a way I was too young to read *The Story of the Treasure Seekers*. I was at one with the children – I had a naive child's reaction to the story. Like them, I thought they had really found treasure rather than the uncle deliberately planting silver coins for them to find. It wasn't until I read it to my own daughter years later that it clicked.'

Wilson first saw a children's television series of *The Railway Children* before she read it, and entered the drawing competition that followed. 'I tried all afternoon to draw a train but I didn't manage it. In the end I drew the three children waving flags and I won. I never won a prize for writing as a child but I did win an art competition,' she laughs, remembering how as a child she read the first biography of Edith Nesbit by Doris Langley Moore, published in 1933.

Both Edith and Wilson have a deep understanding of what matters to children. Unintentionally, Wilson uses the same description as Edith to explain what it is like to remember being young. 'It's a bit like being an actor,' she says. 'I always write in the first person and I become that child. I find it easier to feel and understand what's troubling them.'

Edith used the idea of being an actor to describe those who accurately remember childhood in her non-fiction work, *Wings and the Child or The Building of Magic Cities*: Edith and Wilson's extraordinary imaginations have created worlds off the page as well as on it. After Edith wrote *The Magic City* she was asked to create a real magic city to go on show at Olympia for readers to see. Likewise, many of Wilson's books have come to life after being dramatized on stage and on the screen, including her story of a Victorian orphan, *Hetty Feather*, not unlike Edith's *Harding's Luck*. An exhibition was held at the Foundling Museum in London, bringing *Hetty Feather* full circle: it was the museum that asked Wilson to write a story about a foundling.

'I've always been interested in anything Victorian, especially children's and adult novels,' says Wilson, who is a collector of the novels by Mrs Molesworth, a contemporary of Edith and one of her influences:

> 'I read my daughter lots of Victorian children's books and we used to visit Victorian houses and look at artefacts and write Victorian stories together. I bought her a Victorian sweet shop and made cardboard characters to go with it. I had my daughter when I was 21 so I was still quite childish and enjoyed playing games.'

Wilson and Edith finally collided in 2012 when Wilson wrote *Four Children and It*, about a modern family who discover the Psammead in a giant sandpit in the woods on holiday. Wilson borrowed the idea from Edith, just as Edith borrowed ideas for her novels from other writers. *Four Children* is a warm, contemporary and thoughtful update of the Psammead story as two somewhat old-fashioned children Rosalind and Robbie are forced to spend the summer with their ultra-modern, selfish step-sister Smash and sweet half-sister Maudie. The characters ring true, with the children's modern wishes being both different and the same as their Victorian counterparts – from becoming famous to climbing trees, being able to fly and writing a bestseller. The two novels cleverly and magically collide when Rosalind wishes to meet the original children, Anthea, Robert, Jane, Cyril and the Lamb. Just like Edith's novel, the fun of the plot is that the wishes don't turn out as the children expect.

And what if Wilson met the Psammead? What would she wish for? 'I would like to see for myself what E. Nesbit was like,' says Wilson:

'I would probably ask her if she found it a delight or not to answer all the lovely letters she received from her readers. I'd be a bit scared of her I think. She seems quite formidable. Maybe if we became ultra buddies over a bottle of wine I'd ask her how she could bear to bring up Alice's children. It was quite an extraordinary thing to have done. I'd love to know if she really did it out of love for Hubert, who doesn't seem to be much of a lovable person at all.

'I think she had quite a quick temper, and she acted rather grandly. When she writes about writers, such as the Mother in *The Railway Children*, they are always seen as magnificent. Did she really see herself as splendid and wonderful all the time? But I also think how gamely she managed her reduction in circumstances when she married her second husband and still continued to entertain in style. She was brave in those class conscious times in getting together with a man who was beneath her socially.

'She was a very bold lady pursuing various young men. She was a real tomboy and was in her element playing boyish games.

'She is a most interesting character and bits and pieces off her work have stayed with me always.'

With *Four Children and It* due to be made into a film starring Michael Caine as the voice of the Psammead, Jacqueline Wilson could be considered as a contemporary Edith Nesbit. She is a writer for children who refuses to patronise her readers and instead conjures up worlds where magic and realism collide for vivid, true characters in unforgettable stories that will stay with young readers for the rest of their lives.

The Railway Children, 1970. The cast of the beloved film say goodbye.

Edith's Guide to Life

'Very wonderful and beautiful things do happen, don't they? And we live most of our lives in the hope of them.'
The Railway Children

'The magic of the imagination…is the best magic in the world.'
Wings and the Child or The Building of Magic Cities

'Children are like jam: all very well in the proper place
but you can't stand them all over the shop.'
The Would-Be-Goods

'Of course, we are all pleased to suffer for the sake of others,
but we like them to know it.'
The Phoenix and the Carpet

'Girls are just as clever as boys and don't you forget it.'
The Railway Children

'That's the worst of the truth. Nobody ever believes it.'
The Phoenix and the Carpet

'It is wonderful how quickly you get used to things, even the most astonishing.'
Five Children and It

'It is the most dreadful thing to want to do something for people who are unhappy, and not know what to do.'
The Would-Be-Goods

'I only ask you to remember how hard it is to be even moderately good, and how easy it is to be extremely naughty.'
Nine Unlikely Tales

'She had the power of silent sympathy… It means that a person is able to know that you are unhappy, and to love you extra on that account, without bothering you by telling you all the time how sorry she is for you.'
The Railway Children

'Ladylike is the beastliest word there is.'
The New Treasure Seekers

50 of the Best Works by E. Nesbit

1885   *The Prophet's Mantle*, with Hubert Bland under the name Fabian Bland, Henry J. Drane (novel).

1886   *Lays and Legends,* Longmans, Green & Co (poetry).

1892   *Lays and Legends, Second Series,* Longmans, Green & Co (poetry).

1893   *Grim Tales* and *Something Wrong*, A.D. Innes and Co (ghost stories).

1894   *The Girls' Own Birthday Book*, Henry J. Drane.

1894   *The Butler in Bohemia,* with Oswald Barron, Henry J. Drane.

1895   *A Pomander of Verse*, John Lane (poetry).

1896   *In Homespun*, John Lane (novel).

1897   *The Children's Shakespeare* and *Royal Children of English History*, Raphael Tuck & Son.

1899   *Pussy and Doggy Tales*, Marcus Ward & Co. (children's collection).

1899   *The Secret of Kyriels*, Hurst & Blackett (novel).

1899   *The Story of the Treasure Seekers*, T. Fisher Unwin.

1900   *The Book of Dragons*, illustrated by H.R. Millar, Harper Bros.

1901   *Nine Unlikely Tales for Children*, illustrated by H.R. Millar, T. Fisher Unwin.

1901   *Thirteen Ways Home*, Anthony Treherne & Co (short stories).

1901   *The Would-Be-Goods*, illustrated by Arthur H. Buckland, T. Fisher Unwin.

1902   *Five Children and It,* illustrated by H.R. Millar, T. Fisher Unwin.

1903   *The Literary Sense*, Methuen & Co (short stories).

1903   *The Rainbow Queen and Other Stories*, illustrated by May Bowley, Raphael Tuck & Son.

1903   *The Red House*, Methuen & Co. (novel).

1904   *The Phoenix and the Carpet*, illustrated by H.R. Millar, George Newnes.

1904   *Cat Tales* with Rosamund Bland, Ernest Nister.

1904   *The New Treasure Seekers*, T. Fisher Unwin.

1905   *The Rainbow and the Rose*, Longmans, Green & Co. (poetry).

1905 *Oswald Bastable and Others*, illustrated by H.R. Millar, Wells, Gardner, Darton & Co.

1905 *Pug Peter*, Alfred Cooke, Leeds and London (a dog story).

1906 *Man and Maid*, T. Fisher Unwin (short stories).

1906 *The Story of the Amulet*, illustrated by H.R. Millar, T. Fisher Unwin.

1906 *The Railway Children*, illustrated by C.E. Brock, Wells, Gardener, Darton & Co.

1906 *The Incomplete Amorist*, Constable & Co. (novel).

1907 *The Enchanted Castle*, illustrated by H.R. Millar, T. Fisher Unwin.

1908 *Jesus in London*, illustrated by Spencer Pryse, A.C. Fifield (poem).

1908 *Ballads and Lyrics of Socialism*, published for the Fabian Society, A.C. Fifield.

1908 *The House of Arden*, illustrated by H.R. Millar, T Fisher Unwin.

1909 *These Little Ones*, illustrated by Spencer Pryse, George Allen & Sons (short stories).

1909 *Harding's Luck*, illustrated H.R. Millar, Hodder & Stoughton.

1909 *Daphne in Fitzroy Street*, George Allen & Sons (novel).

1909 *Salome and the Head*, illustrated by Spencer Pryse, George Allen & Sons (a novel).

1909 *Cinderella*, Sidgwick & Jackson (a play with songs).

1910 *The Magic City*, illustrated by H.R. Millar, Macmillan & Co.

1911 *The Wonderful Garden,* illustrated by H.R. Millar, Macmillan & Co (novel).

1911 *Dormant*, Methuen & Co (novel).

1912 *The Magic World*, illustrated by H.R. Millar and Spencer Pryse, Macmillan & Co (short stories).

1913 *Wet Magic*, illustrated by H.R. Millar, T. Werner Laurie.

1913 *Wings and the Child or The Building of Magic Cities*, Hodder & Stoughton.

1914 *Battle Songs*, chosen by E. Nesbit (Max Goschen).

1914 *Children's Stories from English History*, Raphael Tuck & Son.

1921 *The Incredible Honeymoon*, Hutchison & Co (novel).

1922 *The Lark*, Hutchison & Co (novel).

1923 *Five of Us – and Madeline,* T. Fisher Unwin (short stories, linked together by Rosamund).

Sources

The main primary sources I have used are the archives of Doris Langley Moore and Julia Briggs, which are held at the Edith Nesbit Collection held by the Department of Special Collections, McFarlin Library, The University of Tulsa, Oklahoma, United States of America. It is with courtesy and appreciation that the Collection is used as a source throughout the book. Doris Langley Moore's archive includes correspondence between Mrs Langley Moore and Edith's friends, family and colleagues during Mrs Langley Moore's research for her biography between 1931 and 1933, along with notebooks of interviews she conducted and a card index of her notes. Julia Briggs' archive includes notebooks and correspondence during her research for her biography, which was published in 1989. Material from Jocelyn Nixon, the niece of Mrs Paul Bland, is also included in the collection at The University of Tulsa and includes a family photograph album, notebooks of poems, press cuttings and a scrapbook made by Mavis Carter.

Edith's letters to H.G. Wells are among the Wells Papers in the University Library of Illinois at Urbana-Champaign.

I have used resources from the British Library, the Royal Greenwich Heritage Trust (Greenwich Heritage Centre), the Bodleian Library of the University of Oxford, East Sheen Library and the Information and Reference Library in Richmond, TW9.

Other reading material included:
BELL, Anthea, *E. Nesbit: A Bodley Head Monograph*, The Bodley Head, 1960
BYATT, A.S., *The Children's Book*, Chatto & Windus, 2009
CASSON, John, *Lewis and Sibyl – A Memoir*, Collins, 1972
CHESTERTON, Mrs Cecil, *The Chestertons*, George G. Harrap & Company, 1941

COLE, Lesley, *The Life of Noël Coward*, Penguin, 1978

COWARD, Noël, *Present Indicative: The First Autobiography of* Heinemann, 1937

CRESSWELL, Helen, *The Return of the Psammead*, BBC Children's Books, 1992

DAY, Barry, *The Letters of Noël Coward*, New York: Vintage Books, 2009

EAGER, Edward, *Half-Magic*, Houghton Mifflin Harcourt, 1954

EVANS DE ALONSO, Joan, *E. Nesbit's Well Hall, 1915-1921: A Memoir*

HUNT, Peter, *An Introduction to Children's Literature*, Oxford University Press, 1997

JEPSON, Edgar, *Memories of An Edwardian and Neo-Georgian*, Richards, 1937

Oxford Dictionary of National Biography, Oxford University Press, 2004

ROWLING, J.K., *Fantastic Beasts and Where to Find Them*, Bloomsbury (2016)

ROWLING, J.K., *Harry Potter* series, Bloomsbury Publishing Plc (2014)

SAUNDERS, Kate, *Five Children on the Western Front*, Faber & Faber, 2014

SEAVER, George, *Memories of E. Nesbit,* 14 November 1973

STREATFEILD, Noel, *Magic and the Magician*, Ernest Benn Ltd, 1958

TOMALIN, Claire, *Several Strangers: Writing from Three Decades*, Penguin, 2000

ZIPES, Jack, (editor-in-chief), *The Oxford Encyclopaedia of Children's Literature* volume 3, Oxford University Press, 2006

Publications by The Edith Nesbit Society including newsletters and:

AIKEN, Joan, *In Celebration of Edith Nesbit*, 1998

FRENCH, G.E., *Hubert Bland: A Personal View*, 2006

GRIFFIN, Betty, *Edith Nesbit and The Dinosaurs at Crystal Palace*, 2007

KENNETT, John, *Tommy Tucker: A Look at the Life of the Second Husband of Edith Nesbit, An Illustrated Biography*, 2010

PROBERT, Laura, *The Well Hall Garden Parties*, revised by John Kennett, 2005

PROBERT, Laura, *Which Railway?*, 1999

REED, Nicholas, *Edith Nesbit in South East London and Kent – An Illustrated Biography*, 1997, revised by John Kennett, 2009

Television material including:

The Edwardians play starring Judy Parfitt as E. Nesbit, BBC Television, 1973, written by Ken Taylor.

Five Children and It television series, BBC, 1991.

SOURCES

Interviews including:
Anna Baruma, conducted at Liberty London, March 2017
Jacqueline Wilson, conducted at The Foundling Museum, London, July 2017
Kate Saunders, conducted by telephone and email September 2016
Jenny Agutter conducted by email November 2017
Bernard Cribbins conducted by telephone October 2017

Permissions granted:
The Railway Children stage production facts, figures and interviews reproduced
    with permission from Runway Entertainment.
Five Children and It film adaptation: quotes approved by Capitol Films and the
    UK Film Council in association with the Isle of Man Film Commission
    and in association with Endgame Entertainment. A Jim Henson Company
    Production, A Capitol Films / Davis Films Production.
Paragraph about Oakworth station: with the kind help of the Keighley & Worth
    Valley Railway.
J.K. Rowling (quoted from the website of the publisher Little, Brown): https://
    www.littlebrown.co.uk/authors/detail.page?id=eRNOfibrXEzA1ctynClx
    whOKqUAq5y7YN6hqxjG-JuNDUntFfYOq
Pottermore.com

Exhibitions included: The Golden Age of Children's Literature at St Hilda's
College curated by Laura Kondrataite.

All quotes taken from E Nesbit's children's novels (unless otherwise stated) are
from the 1993 editions published by Wordsworth Classics, www.wordsworth-
editions.com

Notes

Chapter 6

1 Edith's letter to Ada Breakell about George Bernard Shaw, 1885 (probably the summer but undated), with acknowledgement to The Society of Authors, on behalf of the Bernard Shaw Estate.

2 George Bernard Shaw's diary entries: *Bernard Shaw: The Diaries 1885-1897* editor Stanley Weintraub, Pennsylvania State University Press, (1986), with acknowledgement to The Society of Authors, on behalf of the Bernard Shaw Estate.

3 George Bernard Shaw's review of Edith's work in a letter, 18 October (no year), with acknowledgement to The Society of Authors, on behalf of the Bernard Shaw Estate.

4 Letter about poetess asking Shaw to commit adultery: To Molly Tompkins, 22 February 1925, from his *Collected Letters 1911-1925* edited by Dan H Laurence, Frederick Ungar Publishing Co (1985).

Chapter 7

1 8 Dorville Road described in a letter by Eric Bellingham Smith, who was taught by Alice Hoatson with Paul and Iris, 3 August 1966, now in the possession of Mrs Shirley Colqhoun.

2 Oscar Wilde's letter to E. Nesbit, Oscar Wilde to E. Nesbit: found in *The Letters of Oscar Wilde*, ed Rupert Hart Davis, Harcourt (1962). © the Estate of Oscar Wilde 1962.

Chapter 15

1 Letters from H.G. Wells to Edith: the majority that have survived are dated between January 1905 and January 1906, with courtesy of Wells Papers at Illinois: Rare Book & Manuscript Library, University of Illinois at Urbana-Champaign.

2 H.G. Wells' version of events and description of the Blands: *Experiment in Autobiography*, Victor Gollancz Ltd (1932).

3 Letter from Rosamund to H.G. Wells, 12 November 1915 and 3 September (no year), with courtesy of Wells Papers at Illinois: Rare Book & Manuscript Library, University of Illinois at Urbana-Champaign.

Image Credits

Tommy Tucker with parrot: The Edith Nesbit Society Archives
Five Children and It: BBC Photo Library
George Bernard Shaw: Universal History Archive/UIG/Bridgeman Images
Family Tree: Geri Livingston
Jacqueline Wilson: Friends of Well Hall Pleasaunce
John Collis Nesbit: Getty Images
The Railway Children 1970 film: STUDIOCANAL Films Ltd
Hubert Bland: Royal Greenwich Heritage Trust

Front cover image: Mary Evans Picture Library, Getty Images, Copyright © Morris & co., Stylelibrary.com Back cover image: Getty Images
All other images: With courtsey of the Department of Special Collections, McFarlin Library, The University or Tulsa, Oklahoma, U.S.A.

Index

INDEX